INSURANCE LOGIC

INSURANCE LOGIC

Risk Management Strategies for Canadians

Moshe A. Milevsky, Ph.D.
and Aron A. Gottesman, Ph.D.

Stoddart

Published in 2002 by Stoddart Publishing Co. Limited
895 Don Mills Road, 400-2 Park Centre, Toronto, Canada M3C 1W3

Distributed by:
General Distribution Services Ltd.
325 Humber College Blvd., Toronto, Canada M9W 7C3
Tel. (416) 213-1919 Fax (416) 213-1917
Email cservice@genpub.com

10 9 8 7 6 5 4 3 2 1

Canadian Cataloguing in Publication Data

Milevsky, Moshe Arye, 1967–
Insurance logic: risk management strategies for Canadians

ISBN 0-7737-3326-4

1. Insurance, Life — Canada. 2. Risk (Insurance) — Canada.
I. Gottesman, Aaron A. II. Title.

HG179.M516 2002 368.32'00971 C2001-904203-5

This book is for information only and should not be construed as investment advice or a recommendation to buy, sell, or hold any securities. Readers should use their own judgement and/or consult professional advisors for specific applications to their individual circumstances.

Cover design: Angel Guerra
Text Design: Tannice Goddard

The Canada Council for the Arts since 1957 | Le Conseil des Arts du Canada depuis 1957

We acknowledge for their financial support of our publishing program the Canada Council, the Ontario Arts Council, and the Government of Canada through the Book Publishing Industry Development Program (BPIDP).

Printed and bound in Canada

Contents

Acknowledgements

We would like to start by thanking our respective wives, Edna and Ronit, for providing moral support to their husbands, and for their patience during the writing process.

Likewise, Don Bastian and Marnie Kramarich, and especially Gillian Watts, deserve much credit for helping us to undertake and complete this project. Behind every good author there stands a team of editors with whips and chains!

We would also like to thank Jody Engle, Julia Kampis, and Nicolas Salerno for research assistance.

In addition, we would like to thank the following individuals for providing comments, suggestions, and ideas that helped improve the book. They are: Daniel Collison, Kim Wood, Hugh MacKay, Lowell Aronoff, Robert Kienman, Eli Bienenstock, and Glenn Daily.

Finally, we would like to thank our academic colleagues at York University (Toronto) and Concordia University (Montreal) for providing an environment conducive to conducting the research for this book.

Moshe A. Milevsky and Aron A. Gottesman, September 2001

Introduction

You Are Richer Than You Think

Most Canadians worry about money. They worry that their salaries and wages are too low, they worry that their investments aren't growing as fast as they would like, and they worry about taxes and household expenses. Ask typical Canadians to compute their net worth, and they will probably add up the cash in their bank accounts, their RRSPs, personal pensions, and mutual funds, and perhaps the value of their homes (minus the mortgage, of course) and physical possessions, arriving at a quite sobering number — preferably positive.

But this approach to estimating net worth is wrong. Whatever number you get as an answer, you are probably worth 10 to 20 times that amount. If the above exercise gave you a total of $50,000, you are probably worth $500,000, and if you computed $200,000, then you are probably worth $2 million — and possibly more.

"What am I missing?" you ask. In a nutshell, you have focused on your *financial* capital and possessions, but ignored your *human* capital. For most working Canadians, their human capital is worth much more than their financial capital. And once you include your human capital in the equation, you end up with a number that is much larger than the answer you get when you focus on financial capital alone.

Human capital is a measure of your future wages, income, and salary. For example, if you are a doctor, lawyer, engineer, or academic, you probably invested an enormous amount of time, effort, and money in your education. That investment should pay off in many years of income from your productive labour. You could think of yourself as a stock — a share in Me, Inc. — that will pay dividends over the next 10, 20, or even 30 years. How do you list this investment on your personal balance sheet? This potential is your human capital. As Figure I.1 suggests, you are your biggest investment, and you are also the chief financial officer of Me, Inc.

Expanded View of Wealth

Figure I.1

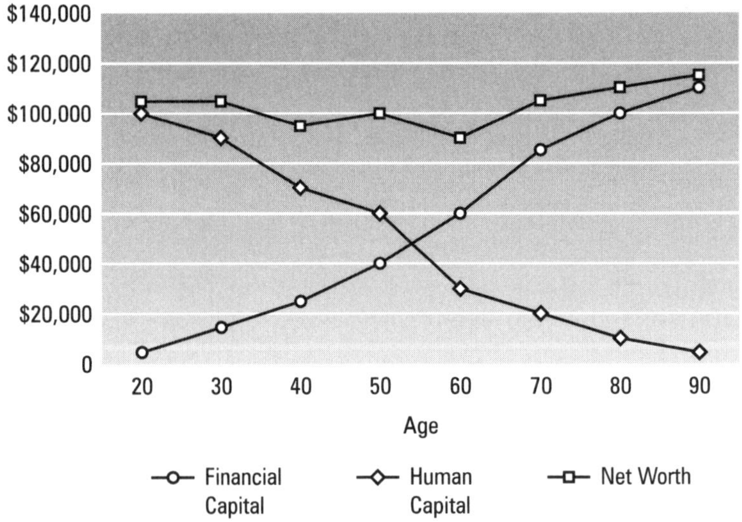

This book is about protecting, managing, and hedging the risks to both your human and financial capital — otherwise known as insurance. Our motivation for writing the book stems from a simple observation. Browse through the personal finance books in your favourite bookstore, and you will notice that almost all of them are devoted to increasing and protecting your financial capital exclusively. There are hundreds of books devoted to mutual funds, stocks, and real estate, written to help you grow and protect the financial aspects of your net worth. Yet very few, if any, are concerned with protecting your human capital. The subject of life, health, and property insurance is not always pleasant to contemplate, but it is critical. This book is an attempt to fill the gap in the popular literature by stressing the importance of protecting *both* your financial and your human capital.

The Agenda for This Book

We recognize that insurance isn't always the most cheerful topic to discuss, and our sympathies go out to people who have to sell it for a living. But we do believe there is a genuine and significant gap in public knowledge about insurance and risk management issues in general. Given the importance of proper risk management in our lives, it's a gap that needs to be filled. We hope this book will take you some distance towards that objective. The following is a brief synopsis of what's ahead.

In Chapter 1 we explore the theoretical principles that underlie the relationship between the providers and holders of insurance, using the context of life insurance as an example. While we focus on life insurance, the principles discussed in this chapter are generic to all insurance products, serving as a foundation for the more type-specific discussions in later chapters. We relate insurance prices to underlying probabilities and potential claims, and then explain why purchasing insurance is implicitly a *hedge*, not an investment. Since it is a hedge, the policyholder must consider the two dimensions of insurance risk — probability of loss and magnitude of loss. We also introduce the concept of adverse selection and discuss the general trade-off that occurs with deductible levels and premiums.

In Chapter 2 we move to the end of the life cycle and introduce readers to the many issues associated with longevity insurance. We begin by describing longevity insurance in detail and then discussing annuitization, the insurance vehicle through which longevity insurance is provided. We explain that the decision whether or not to annuitize liquid assets is difficult, since it is irreversible and can, in hindsight, prove costly. A person must decide whether to annuitize, and if so, when to do so. We proceed to argue that annuitization provides valuable longevity insurance, and should be actively encouraged for older people.

In Chapter 3 we discuss the pros and cons of purchasing private health insurance in general, as well as travel insurance specifically. We begin by reviewing Canada's public health insurance system in the context of the Canada Health Act. We then review health-related services not covered by public health insurance and wade into the politically charged issues of the advantages and disadvantages of Canada's public health insurance system. On the topic of travel insurance, we discuss the role the Canadian government plays in subsidizing health care costs for Canadian travellers abroad — and why it is often insufficient. We also discuss restrictions for pre-existing medical conditions and the impact these restrictions have on private health insurance and travel insurance.

In Chapter 4 we describe both disability insurance and critical illness insurance. We begin by arguing that protection against disability is important, and analyze why many people fail to recognize its importance. We then describe the similarities and differences between the two types of products. We describe how disability plans likely pay more in the long run because they are in the form of a consistent income stream, while critical illness plans pay an initial lump sum upon diagnosis. We discuss the advantages and disadvantages of each, and conclude by arguing how attempts to satisfy the dual objectives of income replacement and expense coverage, given cash flow constraints, are satisfied in the context of disability insurance, critical illness insurance, private health insurance, and life insurance.

In Chapter 5 we provide a detailed overview of automobile insurance. Why does automobile insurance cost as much as it does? And why are there such dramatic variations in price between rival companies? These questions have probably crossed the mind of every automobile owner at one time or another. The goal in this chapter is to try to answer these questions and to explain why the prudent consumer is well-advised to do a little comparison price shopping before committing to a specific policy or insurer. We begin by describing the basics of automobile insurance and the car insurance industry. We then discuss no-fault insurance, price dispersion in the automobile insurance industry, and the factors affecting insurance premiums.

In Chapter 6 we discuss the property insurance industry. Surprisingly, many individuals and families fail to insure their homes properly — particularly those who rent. We discuss the two major components of property insurance, protection against perils and protection against personal liability. We describe the basic choices the consumer must make when buying property insurance: how much insurance to purchase, how high the deductible should be, and which assets to schedule.

In Chapter 7 we familiarize the reader with the many intricacies of dealing with insurance companies. We explore characteristics of the insurance contract that are not contained in its fine print, but are likely to play an important role in determining whether your claim is successful. From choosing an insurance company through to making the claim, failure to recognize the rules by which the insurance industry plays can be expensive. We consider why "cheap" insurance may actually be very costly when it comes time to submit a claim. We consider the insurance company's reputation in the context of whether it satisfies claims as promised and its probability of insolvency. We also discuss choosing an intermediary and making a claim.

In Chapter 8 we discuss the unsavoury practice of insurance fraud. This chapter surveys the extent to which Canadian policyholders practise insurance fraud, and the impact that insurance fraud has on premiums. As well, we explore the moral, legal, and financial reasons why insurance fraud is a very poor idea, and the mechanisms through which the insurance industry, government, and police fight insurance fraud. Finally, this section discusses fraudulent practices by insurance providers and intermediaries — some illegal and some that use legal loopholes — and how consumers can avoid falling victim to fraud.

After some concluding thoughts, we list some additional sources of information and provide a glossary to further assist the reader.

1

Life Insurance and the Theory of Insurance

"Don't take a chance!" screams the latest piece of junk mail you've received. "For only three dollars per week, you can rest assured that you'll be fully protected!"

It seems to us lately that we have been inundated with offers to buy insurance policies against everything from bad weather on our next vacation to veterinarian care for our house pets. You name the calamity, either imaginary or real, and we are willing to bet that some insurance company would love to take that risk right off your shaky hands.

With the relatively minor-sounding premiums — "less than a coffee a day" — how does a rational consumer go about deciding what to insure and what to ignore? The distress factor is very one-sided. If something goes wrong, you will certainly regret not having the insurance. But if nothing happens, you forfeit only a few dollars.

It all comes down to why you buy insurance. In our view, there are two types of insurance consumers. The "insurance for consumption" buyer is looking for peace of mind. To him, insurance is about tranquility; it's like soothing herbal tea or a back massage — just another consumption good. In our opinion, this is not a great way to go about buying insurance. Obviously, if we are talking about a few dollars in premiums per year, it might be no worse than buying lottery tickets for their entertainment value. But the odds favour neither lottery tickets nor insurance for consumption.

In contrast, the "insurance for protection" buyer looks at the purchase from a more rational perspective of risk management. The buyer knows it is not a good investment per se, but if the protection is critical, she is willing to pay the price. What do we mean by "not a good investment"? Well, when you buy a mutual fund, a stock, or a bond, you expect to make money, because those securities pay dividends, interest, and capital gains over time. However, when you buy an insurance policy, you shouldn't expect to make money from it.

Risk and Probability

Figure 1.1

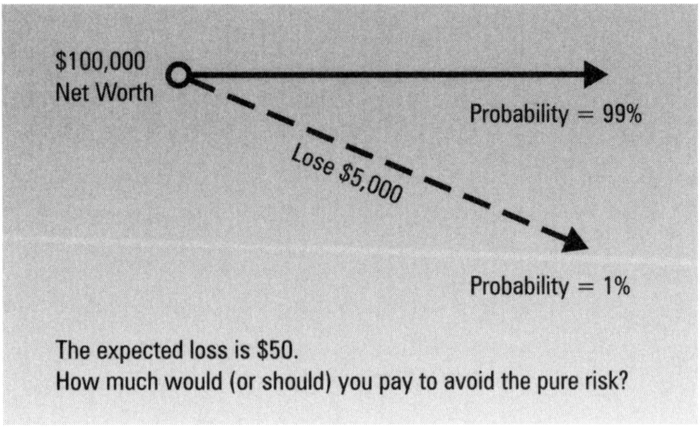

Risk and Probability

Imagine that your net worth is $100,000 and that you own an antique vase worth $5,000 (5% of your net worth). You would like to insure the vase in case it breaks. The insurance company or agent estimates that, in any given year, 1% of precious antique vases are broken. So they multiply the 1% chance by the $5,000 value of the vase, arriving at a pure insurance premium of $50. By *pure* we mean that it comes from simply multiplying the probabilities by the potential damages. No mention is made of costs, profits, commissions, and so on. If, in theory, the insurance company were to sell a hundred of these policies for $50 each, they would have revenues of $5,000, which would exactly pay for the one person (1%) who broke his or her vase. Figure 1.1 should help with understanding this point.

This is the underlying principle of insurance pricing. The pure premium is determined by balancing cash inflows and expected outflows. The insurance company makes sure to sell enough policies to have enough funds to pay claims on an ongoing basis. If they were to sell only one of these vase policies for $50, if and when your vase broke, they would not have enough to pay, even though they had priced it correctly.

From a pure pricing point of view, the insurance company has to account for the probability of the event — the vase breaking — occurring 1% of the time, and they have to make sure they sell enough policies so that they can diversify the risk associated with the payouts they have guaranteed.

As we've said, this doesn't account for any profits, fees, or commissions. So they must clearly charge more than $50 for this policy. In some cases, it could cost 10% to 50% more to cover these additional costs. What this means from a consumer's point of view is that *you are always expected to make less than what you pay in premiums*. You may pay $60, for example, but expect to make only $50.

What do we mean by "expect to make only \$50"? Well, if there is a 1% probability that your vase will break during the next year, then there is a 1% probability that you will get \$5,000. Hence, you *expect* to make 1% of \$5,000, which equals \$50. In most cases you don't receive anything at all — because your vase doesn't break — and in a small percentage of cases you will make \$5,000. But, on average, you expect to make \$50.

Some of you might argue that you never really make anything at all, since your vase has to break in order to get the money. That is obviously true. But in terms of a pure investment, you are investing \$60 in the expectation of making only \$50. That is a lousy investment. So why do it?

The answer is, *because insurance is a hedge, not an investment*. A hedge is a strategy designed to offset financial risks. Your insurance will pay off when your assets suffer a loss. In other words, the loss on the assets is offset exactly by the gain from the insurance benefits. If you've insured properly, your insurance should pay off exactly the amount you have lost. We call this *negative correlation*. Your insurance investment is negatively correlated with your assets. If your assets suffer a loss (the vase breaks), then the insurance will pay off. Insurance is purchased for its hedging properties, not its return properties.

So, if you are the "insurance for consumption" type, there is little we can suggest in terms of logical decision-making. Your insurance purchases will be determined by exposure to marketing and by your own vulnerability. Good luck, and we hope you are not on too many mailing lists. However, once you understand that insurance is a lousy investment but a great hedge, we hope you will become the "insurance for protection" type. Then, when you want to make a rational decision, we believe your focus should be on two issues.

First, ask yourself, "What is the probability of the ill-fated event occurring?" And second, "What is the relative magnitude of the financial loss, if indeed it happens?" If the answer to the former question is "very small," *and* the answer to the latter question is "very large," then by all means buy the insurance. Otherwise, stay away.

Figure 1.2 provides a graphical illustration of the two factors, or what we like to call the two dimensions of insurance risk.

Classification of Pure Risk

Figure 1.2

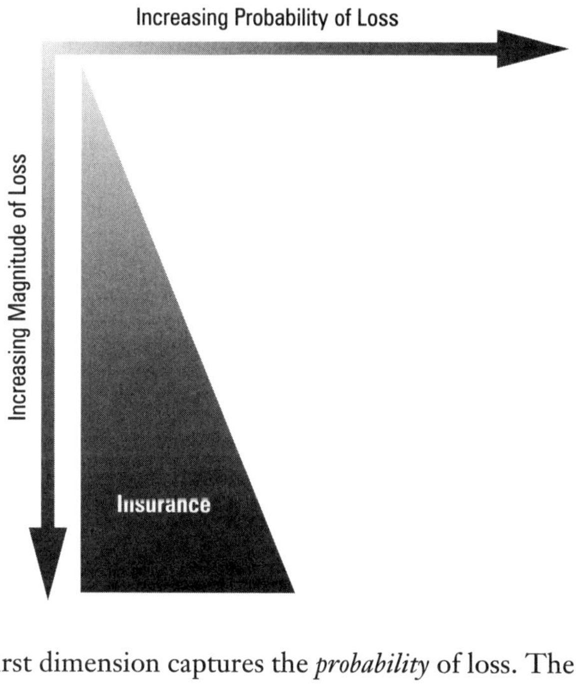

The first dimension captures the *probability* of loss. The smaller this probability, the more important it is to have insurance coverage. Conversely, the greater the probability, the less important it is. After all, as the loss becomes more certain, there is no need to insure as the event is certain to occur. For example, you don't insure against being hungry or requiring new clothes. They might all be costly events. But there is no point in sharing and pooling those risks, since everyone is faced with the same risk.

Life Insurance

While these ideas apply to all insurance products, let's explore them in the context of one specific type of insurance, life insurance. Think of the way a standard (10-year term) life insurance policy works. You pay in a relatively small monthly premium in exchange for a very large payout to your beneficiary or estate in the event of your death. The *probability* of dying during the next few years might be extremely small (say, 1 in 10,000), but the *magnitude* of loss is enormous. If you die, your family will lose the many years of income that you would have earned until retirement and beyond — your human capital, as discussed in the Introduction. This magnitude, which can amount to millions of dollars, is very large, so the need for life insurance falls in the lower left-hand corner of Figure 1.2. You should buy insurance to cover this risk.

This might seem like a very cold and detached way of looking at the value of a human life. After all, humans are worth far more than the value of our future wages and pensions. We would give many millions of dollars to bring our loved ones back, much more than what they could have earned or the value of their pensions. But the single most important lesson about life insurance is that it is meant to financially protect your loved ones upon your passing, not to compensate them for the psychological pain associated with your demise. No sum of money can do that.

Table 1.1 presents the probability of dying within 10 years for people aged 30 through 80.

Table 1.1
What Is the Probability of Dying During the Next 10 Years?

Current Age	Female	Male
30	0.5%	0.9%
40	1.0%	3.0%
50	3.0%	6.0%
60	9.0%	16.0%
70	22.0%	35.0%
80	50.0%	66.0%

Source: Statistics Canada, 1996.

As you can see from the table, the probability of dying during the next 10 years is roughly 70 to 100 times higher at age 80 than at age 30. An 80-year-old female faces a 50% probability of dying during the next 10 years. Effectively, this means that half of the 80-year-old females alive today will not survive 10 years. A sad thought, but does that mean that an 80-year-old female should have a huge life insurance policy, since she is quite likely to die soon? No, absolutely not! Why not? Because the *magnitude* of her loss is very small. After all, the present value of her employment income is close to zero.

Remember, if you die during your thirties, forties, or fifties, your family loses many years of your human capital — your future lifetime earnings. The relative magnitude of this financial loss can be enormous, and devastating. But once you have reached your seventies and eighties, the financial value of your future income is greatly reduced. Therefore, the relative magnitude of loss is much lower as well. Early in life, the probability of loss is generally small but the relative magnitude of loss is large, while later in life, the probability of loss is large but the relative magnitude is small. So you have to balance these two dimensions — the probability and the magnitude. These are the critical ingredients of prudent risk management.

Once again, we don't want to trivialize and reduce the value of human life to a number. No number can compensate for the loss of a loved one. The issue at hand is risk management. Are you putting your young and growing family in financial danger by not insuring yourself? The answer is yes.

As you age, the value of your human capital declines and is usually converted into financial capital. During your working life, you manufacture money by spending effort. You want to insure all the effort you will be investing during your working years, which is precisely why you purchase life insurance. Figure 1.3 illustrates this point in a graphical manner.

How Much Are You Worth?

Figure 1.3

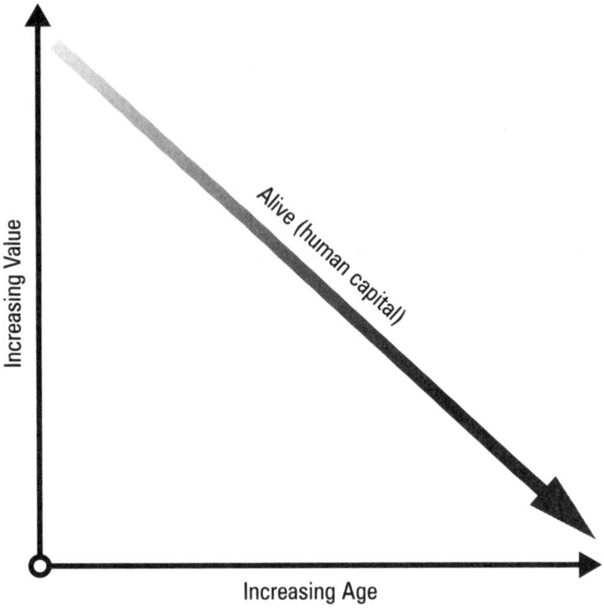

On the horizontal axis of Figure 1.3 is your age, while the vertical axis shows the value of your human capital. Imagine that you have just graduated from school and are about to embark on a career. You have many productive work-years ahead of you, so the value of your human capital is quite high. Of course, if you have a family to support, then you want to protect that human capital (for them) by purchasing life insurance. We will get to the question of how much life insurance in a minute. For now, simply remember, as the above figure indicates, that your human capital declines over time.

So what is the lesson about insurance policies? Remember, no product is sold at cost, for zero profit. Your premiums are, in fact, much higher than what the company expects to pay out, because it is in the business of generating returns for its shareholders. But personal risk management is about protecting you and your loved ones against unsustainable financial losses. In other words, despite the costs, you and your family benefit in the long run. On the other hand, most of those nickel-and-dime policies that are meant to cover relatively small financial losses are most likely a waste of good premium money.

In theory, the insurance premium should reflect the (discounted) value of the insurance benefit, adjusted for the probability that the insurance "event" might occur. In reality, however, price is not so neatly related to the value of insurance benefits. This is because of *asymmetric information* problems between policyholders and insurance providers. Joseph Stiglitz won the 2001 Nobel Prize in Economics for stressing the importance of information asymmetries in economics and insurance theory. The role of asymmetric information in the insurance company/policyholder relationship is as follows: The insurance company may be unable to distinguish clearly between high-risk and low-risk policyholders. It may think that a young male driver is likely to take more risks than a 50-year-old woman, but that's a general perspective. When it comes to two specific individuals, the reality may be quite different. Because of this information gap, the insurance company charges a single premium to all first parties (policyholders) in a certain class, for example, those in a specific age, gender, or geographical group. And typically, the premium charged will be somewhere in the middle of its risk assessment analysis.

The implications of this price-it-in-the-middle approach are obvious. Effectively, low-risk first parties will be overcharged when they purchase insurance, while high-risk first parties will be undercharged. As a result, if buying additional coverage is an option (not mandatory), then more high-risk consumers will purchase insurance than low-risk consumers. After all, they're getting a bargain. *This effect is known as adverse selection.* The insurance company may be taking on more risk than initial estimates of the population would suggest, because it will have a disproportionate number of high-risk clients. This could place the company in a potentially ruinous situation, since it will have to pay out more claims than it expects.

Adverse selection also suggests that information asymmetries may result in some policyholders overpaying for life insurance while others underpay. Hence, the resulting price-it-in-the-middle approach diverges from the "fair" price of the insurance — the present value of expected future cash flows.

Let's consider an example. An insurance company decides to market a new life insurance policy to females between the ages of 45 and 55. Analysts have determined that the typical female of that age has a 0.1% chance of dying in any given year. Based on that mortality rate, and assuming that the face value of the policy is $100,000, the company decides to charge $100 in annual premiums for individuals in the target group.

Imagine, for a moment, that there are two types of females:

- those more likely to die, who have an associated annual mortality rate of 0.15%. Individuals with such a high mortality rate should pay $150 for the insurance being offered.
- those less likely to die, with an associated annual mortality rate of 0.05%. Individuals with such a low mortality rate should pay $50 for the insurance being offered.

Thus, for high-risk policyholders, the premium of $100 is a bargain: $50 ($150 – $100) cheaper than expected. On the other hand, low-risk policyholders are paying $50 ($100 – $50) *more* than expected. Hence, more high-risk individuals will purchase the life insurance.

In the above example, note that adverse selection occurs because low-risk policyholders can choose whether or not to purchase the insurance. This is an important consideration; for adverse selection to occur, three general conditions must be met:

1. The consumer has information about his or her own risk profile that the insurance company is unaware of.
2. The consumer is more likely to enter into the insurance contract when the risk level is high.
3. The consumer has the right to turn down the offer to purchase insurance.

The first condition reflects the existence of asymmetric information in situations where adverse selection occurs. If this information gap did not exist, the insurer could accurately price the insurance contract it signs with each policyholder, based on a discount of the expected future cash outflow. Again, while it is possible to classify policyholders on the basis of age, habits, geographical location, and other variables, it is impossible to know fully the risk characteristics of each consumer.

The second condition reflects the fact that adverse selection occurs because high-risk consumers are more likely than low-risk consumers to accept the contract. This skewed motivation will change the risk profile of the typical policyholder. The third condition suggests that adverse selection is an issue only when low-risk policyholders have the option to refuse the insurance contract.

While discussing adverse selection, let's mention another concept — *moral hazard*. The concept of moral hazard refers to situations in which an individual behaves recklessly, knowing that the insurance company can't observe the behaviour and that therefore he or she will not incur the cost of the reckless behaviour.

Of course, once they are insured, policyholders do not immediately engage in reckless behaviour! Potential reckless behaviour is restrained by the risk of large costs to the policyholder should an accident take place. These personal costs could range from major physical harm to the legal and financial difficulties associated with filing a claim.

Although this does not apply in the context of life insurance, another way to reduce moral hazard is by charging a high deductible. For example, as we will discuss in Chapter 5, insurance companies can charge lower premiums for automobile insurance policies that have larger deductibles. While it's wrong to say that the deductible, and the deductible alone, acts to mitigate moral hazard, the larger it is, the greater the monetary costs to the policyholder should he or she behave recklessly. We would then expect to see a negative relationship between the size of the deductible and reckless behaviour.

How Much Life Insurance Do You Need?

There are two approaches to determining how much life insurance a person requires. One is the income approach and the

How Much Insurance Do You Need?

Figure 1.4

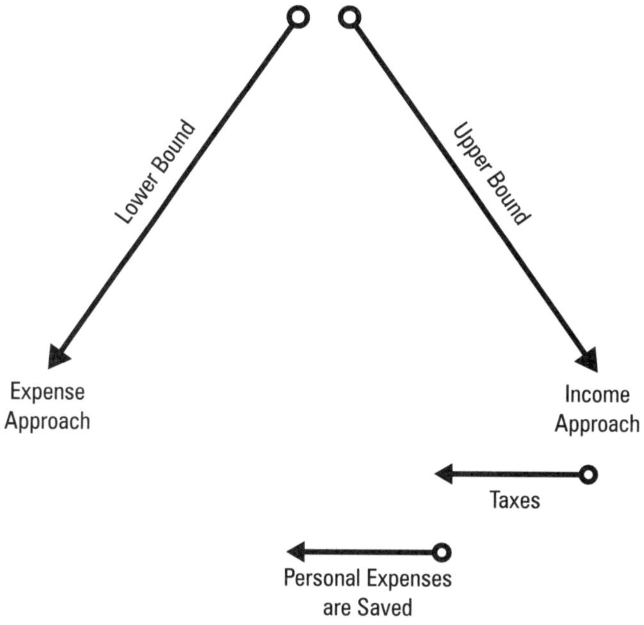

other is the expense approach. Figure 1.4 illustrates the relationship between the two approaches.

The first approach is the *income approach*, which looks at how much money you can expect to earn over the course of your working life, subtracts taxes (since the death benefit is typically not taxable), subtracts the expenses you would have incurred had you been alive, and sets that as the amount of insurance you require.

The second approach is the *expense approach*. This method looks at the expenses your family will incur over the course of their lives. You then buy insurance to cover those expenses rather than to replace your income. As you can imagine, there will be a wide variation between the amounts of insurance you think you need if you use the (family) expense method as opposed to the income approach. And the wealthier you are and the larger your income, the larger this gap will be.

Thus, for example, if you make $100,000 per year, and if you expect this number to remain fairly constant in real terms (after inflation) for the rest of your life, the income approach might lead to about $1 million in life insurance coverage, which could be the present (discounted) value of your income at some interest rate (this calculation has a lot of mathematics and spreadsheets behind it). The expense approach would compute the cost of living for your family, such as food expenses and putting your kids through school, which might be only $500,000. Thus, any amount between $500,000 and $1 million would be acceptable as a life insurance policy. We could spend the next three pages doing a case study of John Doe's expenses and income, but we hope you get the point without that. Before you get life insurance, sit down and do an analysis of your income and expenses — preferably before you meet the insurance agent or broker. The process will be quite revealing.

This brings us to another important concept of insurance. Although pricing of insurance is a rigorous and scientific discipline, determining the amount of insurance coverage that you require is not. Many people mistakenly believe that you can never have too much insurance. Many in the insurance industry would certainly want you to believe that as well. We disagree. We think that there is an upper bound (the income approach) and a lower bound (the expense approach), and anything in between is fair game. We'll leave it to you and your insurance agent to work it out.

Remember, insurance is a lousy investment, but a great hedge — but don't overhedge. You would probably be better off putting the excess premiums in the bank or in a mutual fund, because you would end up with more in the long run than if you put the money into insurance premiums. (This is certainly true on a pre-tax basis. We will address the tax quirks later.)

You will notice that, regardless of whether you take the income or the expense approach, your insurance needs will change over time. Obviously, your family's expenses will decline substantially as your children grow up and leave the nest. Likewise, the discounted value of your wages and other income will decline with time. So there is really no justification for buying more and more life insurance as you age.

Types of Life Insurance Policies

There are two basic categories of life insurance, which go under the odd names of *temporary* and *permanent*. The two are quite different approaches to insuring yourself, and it's important to understand the nuances.

Temporary life insurance, which also goes under the name of *term life*, is a no-frills way of insuring yourself for a specific period of time — for example, one, five, or ten years. Your monthly premiums are guaranteed for the term of the insurance, and at the end of the term, the insurance coverage ends. If you survive to the end of the period — and we certainly hope you do — then the policy is worthless. If, on the other hand, you die during the time period, your beneficiaries will receive the face value of the policy. Once the term of the insurance is over, you might want to get another insurance policy for another term, and so the process continues.

The important characteristic of a term policy is its temporary nature, as well as the fact that it has no savings component. This might seem an odd comment at first, since insurance should have nothing to do with savings. But you will see in a moment that permanent life insurance does have a savings component.

Temporary coverage, as its name suggests, is great for temporary needs. For example, if you have just purchased a house and financed it with a large mortgage, you might want some temporary insurance to cover the liability in case something unfortunate happens to you over the life of the mortgage. Temporary insurance makes sense for young couples who have growing children, or if the family would face a serious financial crisis if something were to happen to the primary breadwinner. Remember, the value of your human capital is considerable earlier in your life, and you want to protect it. We envision the young couple having a substantial amount of term life insurance while the children are young, perhaps eight to ten times their annual salaries. As they age, it can be reduced to six to eight times the annual salaries, and then perhaps even to four to six times.

Of course, as you age and renew your term insurance, the premiums will increase. Why? Well, the probability of dying increases, so the insurance company must charge more to cover this risk. Does that mean you need more life insurance — because you are more likely to die? No, not at all. As we explained earlier, you must consider two dimensions: the probability of loss, which increases as you age, and the magnitude of loss, which declines as you grow older. So we argue that, all in all, the older you are, the less coverage you need. Remember also that insurance gets more expensive as you age — another argument for having less as time goes on.

If and when you buy temporary, or term, insurance, make sure to get a policy that has a *guaranteed renewable* clause. This means that, even if your health deteriorates, when the original period is over, you can purchase a replacement policy without having to undergo a medical examination. When you take out life insurance, the insurance company usually requires you to undergo a medical exam (or at least a blood test) to make sure that you are not more unhealthy than average. They want to make sure — as macabre as this sounds — that you have not been diagnosed with a terminal illness and have only a few months to live, and are buying the insurance simply to make a quick dollar. This might seem like the last thing that would be on your mind at such an unfortunate time, but insurance companies are quite rightfully worried about this; they have to make sure that they are pooling and spreading the risks. Guaranteed insurability is therefore a very important feature of a temporary policy, since it gives you peace of mind knowing that you will be able to renew your coverage, albeit at a higher price.

While a guaranteed renewability clause implies that one no longer requires a medical exam, an exam will likely still be required if you want to *increase* your coverage, and the insurance company could well refuse coverage otherwise. (You may even have to undergo a colonoscopy — an ugly experience indeed!) However, once you pass the medical exam, additional coverage should not be a problem.

When we talk about replacing human capital, we are not talking about replacing only "official" income. Stay-at-home parents, homemakers, and caregivers provide valuable services to the family — services that are costly to replace. One of your authors learned the value of unofficial incomes firsthand. A short time ago, Moshe's wife, Edna, took a two-day vacation and left him to care for his three daughters, whose ages ranged from one to six. Moshe quickly realized how much work the kids could be. Getting them bathed, dressed, fed, and to school, all with no help — what a job! When Edna came home, the first thing Moshe did — after bolting from the apartment — was contact his insurance company and buy some more life insurance on his wife, making him the beneficiary.

So much for temporary insurance coverage. What is permanent coverage? This type of coverage sometimes goes under the name of *whole life*, *universal life*, or *level life* insurance. There are various types and flavours of permanent coverage, but the main idea is that your monthly or quarterly insurance premiums also contain a savings component. So if you pay $100 per month, perhaps $60 goes towards the insurance premiums, while the remaining $40 goes to a side savings fund.

Why the savings? Figure 1.5 provides a good indication of what is happening. With term insurance, your premiums increase each year because the probability of dying increases as you age. In fact, when you are in your seventies and eighties, not only are the premiums prohibitively expensive, but you may not be able to purchase coverage at any price. Level, or permanent, insurance is a system whereby you overpay in the early years in order to subsidize the later years. As you can see from Figure 1.5, level insurance premiums are higher than term premiums for the first part of your life, while term premiums exceed level premiums later on. This is where the savings come in. Since you are overpaying in the early years, the excess over the pure premiums is being invested in a side fund. In some cases, you can actually control where those excess premiums are invested. For example, you may be able to choose to invest in insurance company mutual funds or GICs. As you age, some of the savings will be depleted to make up for the fact that your annual level premiums are lower than what they should be. With these so-called universal policies, you can withdraw, or cash in, the excess savings at any time, so you have access to an emergency fund in times of need.

The Marvellous Tax Angle

As the old saying goes, there is nothing certain in life but death and taxes, and nowhere do the two go more hand in hand than in the life insurance business. Were it not for income taxes, this

Term Versus Level Life Insurance

Figure 1.5

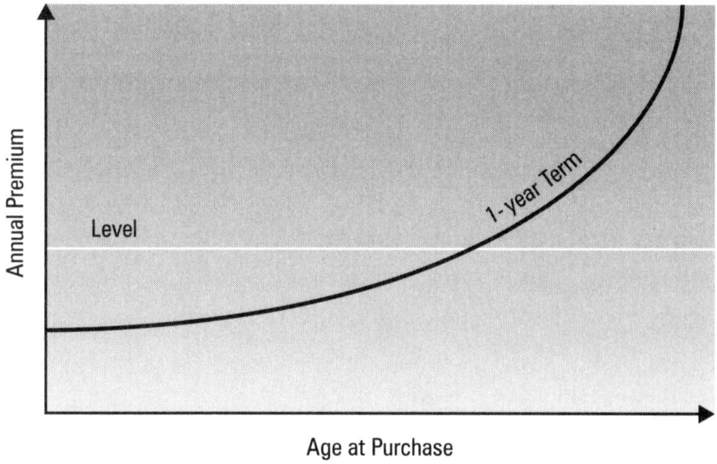

chapter would end right here. There would be two basic types of life insurance, term and permanent (or whole life, universal life, etc.), and the better type for most people — to protect their human capital — would probably be a term policy with guaranteed renewability. Then, towards your retirement years, when your responsibilities and commitments lessen and the value of your human capital dwindles, you would slowly lapse or discontinue the coverage. As odd as this might sound, you wouldn't have much to protect.

However, the tax code changes everything.

Some people buy life insurance simply to cover the taxes when they die. The reason is that, in many cases, the physical assets you own might be subject to taxation upon death. This is especially true if you purchased the assets long ago and they have since appreciated in value. Think of a cottage, for example. You might have bought the cottage for a fraction of what it is currently worth. Yet, at death, your children or estate could be faced with a large tax bill that would force the sale of the cottage in order to pay the taxes on it. In other words, the tax code can force you to sell the very asset that you are paying taxes to inherit. Ugh!

Permanent life insurance can come to the rescue. You buy a life insurance policy so that at death your estate is not forced by liquidity considerations to sell assets in order to raise money. Of course, this makes sense only for physical objects that you don't want liquidated, such as vacation properties, valuable antiques, or a small family business that you want to survive your death. This strategy applies to inanimate, non-liquid objects for which the estate or heirs would have no other way to pay the taxes due. But it would certainly *not* make sense to protect a large stock portfolio, RRSP, or RRIF, for example. In such a case, why not sell some of the stock or mutual funds to pay the taxes? Otherwise, you are simply prepaying your kids' tax bill. If you want to, go ahead, but the net present value of the strategy will be negative.

Nevertheless, insurance can play a role in estate planning, and we urge you to consult an expert financial planner before you make any irreversible and expensive decisions. But there is a more intriguing (and mischievous!) side to life insurance that goes beyond tax reasons.

Let's start with the basics. When you invest $10,000 in a bank's five-year guaranteed investment certificate (GIC), and the GIC pays 5% every year, then interest of $500 will be deposited into your bank account each year. If you are in the 50% tax bracket, which means that you have to pay 50 cents for every additional dollar you earn, then $250 of the $500 in interest payments will have to go to Ottawa and the provinces. The remaining $250 can be reinvested in the same or another GIC and left to grow. For the sake of argument, let's say you can invest again at 5%. The same process happens the next year, whereby you have to pay half of the earned interest in taxes and the remainder can be reinvested. So, at the end of the five years, your effective after-tax rate of return will be 2.5% per annum. Sure, you earned 5% before taxes, but after tax, it was only 2.5%.

And here is another important point. Even though you have invested for five years in a compounding GIC, you still have to pay taxes each and every year on the interest you earn, even though you don't cash in the GIC, remove it from the bank, or use the interest. You are being taxed on the "build-up" inside the GIC. This is a fact of investing, and it applies to mutual funds, term deposits, and any other investments that are held for long periods of time. You pay tax on any gains, whether or not you got a cheque for those gains.

Here is where things get interesting with life insurance. We mentioned earlier that with permanent (non-term) policies, part of the periodic premium goes towards pure insurance coverage, while a portion goes towards a savings component to fund future premiums. You might have wondered, as we did when we first learned about non-term insurance, "Why would I mix savings with a life insurance policy?" Why not pay whatever you have to pay for coverage, and put your money to work elsewhere? Sure, your premiums might increase over time, but you should have interest gains from your investments to pay those premiums.

Well, the answer is taxes. Those savings sitting inside the whole life, universal life, or other cash-value policy are growing *tax deferred*. In contrast to the GIC and its bank-deposited interest that we mentioned earlier, your inside build-up is tax-sheltered. You will therefore not get a tax bill every year for any interest (or capital gains or dividends, for that matter) that you might have earned inside the policy. Once again we reiterate that this is in stark contrast to what happens with a bank deposit or mutual fund, where you get taxed on any gains.

You can't escape tax forever. When you decide to take the cash surrender value of the policy, you will have to pay the taxes, but the savings from not having to pay tax every year can be enormous. Without getting into too much detail, here is a simple example of the immense benefits of the deferral value.

Imagine that you invest $10,000 at 5% interest for 30 years, and the inside build-up is taxed every year at your 50% marginal tax bracket. Each year you pay taxes on any gains. Do the math yourself and you will find that in 30 years you have $20,975. Technically, the calculation is done by raising 1.025 to the power of 30 and then multiplying by the initial $10,000 (the 1.025 comes from the after-tax return).

Now, what happens if the inside build-up is tax-free? In this case, at the end of 30 years you have 1.05 raised to the power of 30, which is $43,220 before taxes are paid — a gain of $33,220. Then you must pay 50% tax on the gain of $33,220, which leaves you with $26,610. (The growth was tax-sheltered, so the interest factor was 1.05 instead of the after-tax amount of 1.025.)

Compare the numbers. You have $5,635 ($26,610 – $20,975) more from the tax-free inside build-up than from the alternative product. This is about 50% of your initial $10,000 investment. Now scale this up to $100,000, or even $500,000, and you get a sense of the magnitude of this benefit. Remember, there is no sleight of hand here. You have paid taxes in both cases, so we are not comparing apples to oranges. In the first case, you paid tax continuously; in the second case, you paid it at the end.

Today you can use this strategy with a large variety of investment funds within a life insurance policy — hence the name universal life. If you hold a fund outside of an insurance policy, you have to pay annual taxes on realized capital gains, dividends, and interest earned by the fund. When they are sitting inside, you can forget about tax for as long as the policy is in force. You could probably pick your favourite Canadian mutual fund and figuratively wrap a life insurance contract around it, thus benefiting from the tax-free inside build-up. Sure, you have to get some life insurance in order to play this game, but that's the price you have to pay — and more insurance may not be a bad thing after all.

Such are the benefits of tax-free inside build-up in a life insurance policy. And if you haven't yet rushed out to the nearest insurance company, here is another titbit that might make you embrace the closest CLU (chartered life underwriter). In some cases, you never have to pay a dime of taxes on any of the gains; you can pull the money out of the policy tax-free.

"How?" you ask. "What's the catch?"

First of all, when you die, your beneficiary receives the proceeds of the policy tax-free. That's pretty obvious — and fair, since you didn't get to deduct the premiums from taxes payable when you bought the policy. But more importantly, you can borrow against the cash value of the policy whenever you want, or at the end of 30 years, for example. When its value has reached the above-mentioned $43,220, instead of cashing in, you can borrow $43,220 (in many cases, from the same insurance company) and thus avoid paying any taxes at all. Your borrowing is secured against the cash value (savings) of the policy, and money you borrow does not create a tax liability.

Let's go through this again just to make sure it's clear. At the end of 30 years — or any time between now and then — you ask the insurance company what your cash surrender value is. But instead of taking the money on the spot in cold, hard cash, thus liquidating or surrendering the policy, you ask them to give you the money — or an equivalent stream of payments — as a loan secured against the policy. Okay, but now you are carrying this big loan on your shoulders. That can't be good, can it?

But the loan is backed by the cash value of the policy. Yes, the interest clock is ticking and you owe the insurance company more and more money each year, but the collateral backing the loan is also growing year after year. When you die and the loan technically comes due, the death proceeds are netted against the outstanding loan — both the loan and the tax liability disappear. As long as the interest rate on the loan is less than or equal to the rate at which your assets are growing inside the insurance policy, you should be fine. Quite clever, we must say.

You might be inclined to buy a lot of whole life insurance that you don't really need for protecting your human capital, just to gain access to the tax-free inside build-up. And we can't really argue with that. On a pre-tax basis it would be silly, but on an after-tax basis — especially if you are paying close to 50% on each additional dollar you earn — this strategy can be a godsend. The possibilities are endless; we know quite a few Ph.D.'s in finance and insurance who work for insurance companies, spending a good part of their days trying to dream up the next great tax arbitrage. And, as one prominent financial planner noted recently when the topic of why these things persist came up, "We have a very powerful insurance lobby in Ottawa."

Tax arbitrage is the science of taking investment positions that capitalize on quirks or inefficiencies in the income tax code. This is both widely practised and legal, and it's up to Ottawa to close these schemes down. But it certainly isn't un-Canadian to take advantage of poor tax-code design. Should these strategies exist? Should life insurance be given a preferential tax treatment? Without getting into an extended policy debate, we think there are merits in giving people incentives to insure themselves and their families. And Ottawa has restricted some of the abuses that existed in the past, such as excessive premium sheltering. But there are still plenty of strategies out there, and in the next chapter we will address one that involves insurance products known as life annuities.

However, before you dump your GICs for universal life policies, you should be cognizant of the fees, expenses, commissions, and charges that might apply on the contract. Many funds inside an insurance policy have higher management expense ratios (MERs) than the same mutual funds outside the policy. Indeed, the enthusiasm with which insurance agents peddle these products, and the large commissions they receive for selling them, make us wonder uncomfortably whether the tax arbitrage gains may be lost in transaction costs, leaving consumers exactly where they started. Nevertheless, the tax benefits stand up to scrutiny. We certainly consider them as a viable savings strategy — if you have used up your RRSP and RESP contribution room, as these are probably better vehicles for most people.

Also, the sheer complexity of the product is a problem in its own right. Most people are simply not equipped with the skills needed to evaluate the cost and benefits of these policies, let alone the conditions under which the strategy makes sense. We have seen many a small business owner buy a million-dollar universal life policy, only to bring their accountant, lawyer, tax specialist, and next-door neighbour (who happens to be a finance professor) to the signing ceremony with the insurance agent, just to make sure that, among all those wonderful minds, somebody understands exactly what is going on. We are firm believers in "Keep it simple, stupid." If it sounds too good to be true, you are probably not listening carefully enough. Don't buy it if you don't understand it.

Finally, if you plan to hold tax-efficient investments such as exchange-traded funds (ETFs), low-cost index funds, or other investment products that try their very best not to declare or distribute capital gains or dividends, you might be able to synthesize your own tax-sheltered inside build-up.

Summary Points

- Any type of insurance is a lousy investment on a pre-tax basis, since the expected "return" is negative in the classical sense. Insurance is purchased for hedging purposes, not investment purposes. The returns from insurance correlate negatively with the returns from your human capital, which implies that insurance hedges your human capital.
- The two most important dimensions for pricing and analyzing life insurance are the probability of the event and the magnitude of the loss. If the probability of the event is large, don't bother paying for insurance, since it is essentially a prepayment plan. The point of insurance is to spread risks that are remote across a large population. If the probability is large, it isn't a risk — it's a certainty. If the magnitude of the event is very small, don't bother with insurance. You can probably afford to suffer the loss, so there is no need to pay the extra fees.
- There are three reasons why insurance markets might break down and you won't be able to get the coverage you need at a reasonable price. The three reasons are (1) small numbers, (2) moral hazard, and (3) adverse selection. A properly designed and fairly priced insurance policy is one that mitigates the effects of all three.
- As you age, the value of your human capital declines. Therefore, all else being equal, the older you are, the less insurance you should have, even though the probability of death increases.
- We are generally skeptical of life insurance policies that are meant to cover taxes due at the time of death. They make sense only under limited conditions, such as when an asset would have to be sold upon death to pay taxes due. Otherwise, they are simply tax-prepayment plans.
- Life insurance is one of the last remaining tax shelters and might be even more powerful than an RRSP in building tax-

favoured wealth. Therefore, even people who don't have the motive of human capital protection for purchasing life insurance might do so for tax purposes. Whether or not this tax break is efficient from a social policy point of view is secondary to the point that it currently exists and should be taken advantage of.

- When you are buying an insurance policy for tax reasons, make sure an expert has gone through the numbers carefully so that you will not lose in commissions and fees anything you might gain in tax savings. And do make sure to compare the returns you are getting — on an after-tax basis — to a low-cost index fund.
- Tax issues associated with an estate motivate some parents to purchase life insurance for their young children when the children have inherited an estate that would otherwise be heavily taxable. Another reason for insuraing young children is to take advantage of guaranteed insurability. Otherwise, we find the practice distasteful and possibly unethical.

How to Sound Intelligent

Questions to Ask When Purchasing Life Insurance

- Is this a term policy or a whole life policy? In other words, does it have any cash value?
- Is my term insurance policy guaranteed renewable at the end of the term without a medical exam?
- If this is a whole life policy, how much of my premium is going to cover the insurance agent's commission and how much is actually going towards life insurance coverage?
- How long do I have to wait before the whole life policy has any cash value?
- What are the total management fees that I will pay on the investments inside the universal life policy, and why are they so much higher than the expenses on my mutual fund?

- Will the universal life policy look attractive on an after-tax basis when compared to a low-cost index fund?
- Do I have a guarantee that I can borrow against the cash value of the life insurance policy at a reasonable rate?

2

Longevity Insurance

Now that Her Majesty the Queen Mother has celebrated a hundred birthdays, some of us wonder about seeing triple digits on a birthday cake during *our* lifetimes. The demographers and actuaries at Statistics Canada don't like projecting that far into the future, but according to them, a large segment of our aging population will be spending more time living in retirement than spending their working years dreaming about it. Health and quality-of-life issues aside, would you be able to afford such a long retirement?

Don't get us wrong. This chapter is not another preachy piece on the virtues of having pre-retirement savings, fully topped-up RRSPs, and the right mutual fund so that you can retire with a nest egg that will feed a tribe. Our concerns deal with the far end of the life cycle and its never-ending doubt about whether you are spending too much.

This is a bigger problem than you might think. No matter how old you are, you will always be worried about spending too much. In the back of your mind you will be wondering, "What if I have 5, 10, or even 15 years to go?" Taking this logic to its extreme, you will never be willing to spend that last dollar. And everybody dies with leftovers! Sure, your kids and your estate lawyer (and perhaps even you) might enjoy the thought of bequests, but you must admit there is a certain inefficiency in consistently depriving yourself today on the chance that there will be a tomorrow. This is quite the double-edged sword. If individuals or couples spend their accumulated savings at too high a rate, they risk outliving their resources. If they spend at too low a rate, they risk suffering an unnecessarily frugal retirement, especially if they die sooner than expected. There is clearly a need to protect against those risks.

To get a better sense of mortality patterns, Table 2.1 illustrates how long people can expect to live. We have chosen the age of 65 as a baseline for retirement, although similar numbers can be generated for any age. The first two columns show the probabilities for an individual female and an individual male, respectively. The last column shows the probability that at least one person from a married couple (both currently aged 65) will survive to the specified age.

In retirement planning scenarios that you might do with a

Table 2.1
Current Age 65 Survival Probabilities

Survival to Age	Single Female	Single Male	At Least One of a Married Couple
70	93.8%	92.0%	99.5%
75	84.4	79.9	96.9
80	70.9	62.7	89.1
85	52.8	41.0	72.2
90	31.6	19.6	45.0
95	13.4	5.8	18.4

Source: RP-2000 Table, Society of Actuaries.

financial planner or advisor, age 85 is the typical assumed life expectancy. But the table shows that at age 85, over 50% of individual females and over 40% of individual males will still be alive. For married couples, at least one of them will still be alive at age 85 in over 70% of the cases.[1] If these survivors had used an 85-year life expectancy to plan their retirement income needs, they would have found that their retirement resources (other than social security) had been used up. This longevity risk — the risk of outliving one's resources — is very substantial and is the reason why we believe that Canadians should consider longevity insurance at some point in their lives.

If you decide to buy longevity insurance from an insurance company (that is, to annuitize), you are transferring the longevity risk to the insurance company. If you decide not to annuitize, you are retaining the longevity risk. Make no mistake about it — longevity risk is real, and should be treated just as seriously as the risk of disability, critical illness, or premature death. The insurance company is in a far better position than you are to hedge and manage those risks. There is, of course, a price. But the main issue we address in this chapter is whether or not you should self-insure against longevity risk.

How Does Longevity Insurance Work?

Another, more common name for longevity insurance is *life annuity*. In its most general form, purchasing a life annuity (whether joint, fixed-term, or single) involves giving a non-refundable lump sum of money to an insurance company in exchange for a monthly or quarterly income stream. With some products, the income ends after a predetermined or fixed period; these are called *fixed-term* or *period-certain* annuities.

1 Please see "Sources and Further Reading" for how these calculations are performed.

With purely life-contingent annuity products, the income ends upon the death of the annuitant or, in some cases, upon the surviving spouse's death.

Obviously, a person can never outlive the income from a life-contingent *immediate annuity* (IA). This so-called lifetime warranty is the essence of longevity insurance. No matter how long he or she lives, no matter how the markets perform, and no matter what happens to interest rates or the economy as a whole, the participant will always get a monthly or quarterly cheque. This is quite similar in concept to the income flow a retiree would receive under a defined benefit pension plan or the Canada Pension Plan.

Annuities, in other words, are a form of longevity insurance — which is the exact opposite of traditional life insurance. Consumers purchase life insurance because they are afraid of dying too soon and thus leaving family and loved ones in financial distress. Consumers buy immediate annuities because they are afraid of living *too long*, so they add income to support the extra years of life.

Table 2.2 lists a number of insurance companies and the monthly payments they provide for longevity insurance to an individual who pays in $100,000 at a number of different ages.

Table 2.2
Monthly Annuity Payments

Insurance Company	Age 60	Age 65	Age 70	Age 75	Age 80
A	$665	$741	$849	$1,002	$1,222
B	650	706	778	890	1,050
C	679	772	891	1,042	—
D	675	752	864	1,026	—
E	667	738	834	983	1,194
F	646	716	816	958	1,160

For example, the table indicates that insurance company A will pay out $665 per month to a 60-year-old who gives them $100,000. If the same individual is 65 years old, he will get $741 per month, and if he is 80 years old, he will get $1,222. All of these payouts last for the rest of the insured person's life. Why the difference based on age? Well, the older the insured person is, the fewer years he or she has to live, and the more the insurance company can afford to pay out. This is the essence of longevity insurance — when you buy the insurance, you are assured that you will have a monthly income stream for the rest of your life.

"How can the insurance company guarantee these payments?" you ask. Here is the nutshell version. Remember the principle of insurance that we mentioned in Chapter 1? By selling policies to many people in the same risk category, the insurance company is able to hedge the risks by diversifying. They might not know how long you are going to live, but if 1,000 individuals buy the coverage, they have a pretty good idea what their customer profile looks like. So the insurers can estimate how much to pay out every month and still get their money back. Of course, when you factor in expenses, commissions, and profits, this may not be an excellent investment on its own, but when combined with the longevity risk we mentioned, it becomes a great hedge. Once again, it's a lousy investment, but a great hedge.

It is important to understand that longevity insurance is more than a fixed-income bond. Here is a simple example that illustrates the annuity concept. According to Statistics Canada, there is a 20% chance that a random 95-year-old female will die during the next year. Equivalently, of a large group of 95-year-old females, 20% of them will not survive for another year. Of course, we do not know exactly which 20% will die.

Now imagine that five such 95-year-old females enter a

legally binding agreement. Each of them contributes $100 to a communal fund that will invest in treasury bills yielding 5%. Then, according to the contract, the surviving females will be entitled to split the proceeds of the fund at the end of the year.

The total contribution of $500 (5 x $100) will grow to $525 by the end of the year. If all five females are still alive at 96 years of age, they will each receive $105, which is the $100 investment plus interest. What happens if one of them — as expected — dies during the next year? Well, the remaining four will be entitled to split the $525, giving each a total of $131.25.

The remaining four survivors will therefore gain a return of 31.25% on their money. If two should happen to die, the remaining three would get $175, which is an impressive 75% return. In other words, the survivors' gains comprise their original principal, their interest, and other women's principal and interest. By pooling mortality risk and ceding bequests, everyone gains. Technically, this agreement is called a *tontine*, also known as a *pure endowment* or *one-period life annuity* contract.

Of course, with only five females in the mortality pool, almost anything could happen. Any combination of them could die, including all of them, or they could all survive. However, if 10,000 such females entered a one-period annuity agreement, it is pretty much assured that the $105,000 would be split among 8,000 survivors. In other words, the expected return from the contract (for the survivors) is 31.25%. The numerator is the total return for the pool and the denominator represents the survivors. The difference between the 5% return available in the market and the 31.25% earned by the survivors is known as *mortality credits*. In addition, the higher the probability of death (that is, the lower the number of survivors), the greater the mortality credits. This same arrangement can be structured over many years, with survivors earning investment returns that depend on how long they live.

The same principle could apply with a variable investment return as well, although they are quite rare in Canada, being mostly available in the United States. In fact, the returns could be even higher. The 10,000 females could invest their $100 in a stock mutual fund that earned 5%, 10%, or even 20%. They would not know in advance what the fund, or pool, would earn. At the end of the year, the annuitants would learn ("realize") their investment returns, and then split the gains among members of the surviving pool. In the event that the investment earned a negative return (lost money), the participants would share in the losses as well, but the effect would be mitigated by the mortality credits. This concept is the foundation of a *variable* immediate annuity, which is the symmetric counterpart to a *fixed* immediate annuity.

Both investments provide longevity insurance via the mortality credits, but with fixed annuities the pool has been invested in fixed-income securities, and with variable annuities it has been invested in variable-return securities, such as stocks and real estate. The choice between fixed and variable immediate annuities is identical to the choice between fixed and variable investment products. Suitable allocations depend on the participant's risk aversion, comfort with fluctuations in the stock market, time horizon, and budget requirements.

In practice, only insurance-chartered companies are allowed to create and manage an agreement in the way we just described in order to provide mortality-contingent products. Most companies go one step further and actually guarantee that you will receive the mortality credit enhancements, even if the mortality experience of the participants is better than expected. In other words, in the above example with an expected 20% mortality rate, the company would guarantee that all survivors would receive 31.25% on their money, regardless of whether or not 20% of the group died during the year. This is how Table 2.2 was constructed.

How can they provide this guarantee? They make very careful and conservative assumptions about the rate of return earned on assets. Furthermore, the greater the number of IAs an insurance company sells or has on its books, the lower the risk of providing this guarantee. These are ultimately economies of scale. In other words, the risks would be significant if they sold only 5 such policies, but with 500,000 policies, the probability of an adverse outcome is close to zero.

Some insurance companies offer products called *participating* annuities. Participants are at risk (or stand to gain) if investment returns or mortality is worse (or better) than estimated. Participating annuities shift a substantial part of the risk from the insurance company to the participant. In some senses, it is akin to the difference between defined-contribution and defined-benefit pension plans. Both are meant to provide a pension, but the risk-sharing mechanism is different.

The Ideal Longevity Insurance Product

In our opinion, any well-functioning retirement or pension plan should have the following features.

- A solid retirement plan should contain a "plain vanilla" fixed immediate annuity that provides a constant, fixed, and dependable monthly income stream for the rest of the participant's natural life. This enables the retiree to hedge the longevity risk that might arise from simultaneously "living too long" and not having enough liquid assets to support consumption.
- The retiree should be able to select a product with a cost-of-living adjustment (COLA) so that payments increase every year by 1% to 5%, depending on the rate selected by the annuitant at the time of purchase. Naturally, the higher

the COLA rate, the more one has to pay at inception, or the lower the monthly payout will be.

- The retiree should have the choice of selecting either a *real* (after-inflation) immediate annuity or a nominal immediate annuity. A real IA will provide periodic payments that increase during inflationary times, while a nominal annuity will not be hedged against inflation. The increase in a real IA differs from a COLA because the former hedges against unexpected inflation, while the latter increases in a predictable manner.
- The IA should provide a choice of various survivorship and certainty periods in order to protect a spouse or dependant by continuing the payment stream beyond the life of the annuitant. For example, the annuitant can elect to have payments continue for 5, 10, 15, 20, or even 25 years, regardless of whether they are alive or not. Once again, the longer or larger the guarantee, the more one has to pay up front, which translates into lower monthly payments.
- During the above-mentioned payment-certain period, during which the death of the annuitant will not disrupt the payment stream, the annuitant should be able to cash out of a portion of the annuity — perhaps with a market-value adjustment or surrender penalty — in order to have access to emergency cash if so desired.
- Although a fixed immediate annuity is of critical importance, the retirement plan should also provide an opportunity to select between fixed and variable IAs, which between them span the risk-and-return frontier in the payout phase. In other words, the participant should be able to pick a suitable asset mix within the immediate annuity. Retirees should be able to invest in any financial asset class or mutual fund either inside or outside the variable IA structure. The retiree can thus seamlessly manage asset allocation decisions

separately from the annuitization decision.

- Given the availability of a variable IA, the participant should have the option of rebalancing, or changing, the asset mix between fixed and variable products during the payout phase, without undue restrictions or penalties. In other words, if the annuitant is so inclined, she can lock or unlock her payment stream at any time during retirement. This is akin to selling some stocks in order to purchase fixed-income bonds, and vice versa, outside of an immediate annuity structure.
- The participant should be able to defer the purchase of an IA until the age of 75, 80, or even 85 if he or she is so inclined. In this scenario the retiree would create a systematic withdrawal plan at retirement — at a rate that satisfies the tax regulations and the minimum distribution requirements — and then annuitize at a more advanced age.
- In addition to the above-mentioned deferred purchase, the participant should have the ability, if he or she so desires, to lock in mortality and interest rates in the IA upon retirement, but with payments that start in 10 or 15 years. This is a true forward-starting IA.
- The participant should be able to compute easily and transparently exactly how much his accumulation will "buy" in the immediate annuity market. This would obviously make budgeting easier and enable the consumer to smooth out fluctuations in lifetime earnings.
- Finally, every individual, regardless of age, should be able to purchase pure longevity insurance that pays a stream of income for the rest of his or her life, starting at any future age, but with no survivor benefits. This is the ideal product where, for example, a 35-year-old pays a few thousand dollars to an insurance company in exchange for a guarantee that, if and when he ever reaches the age of 80, he will

receive a larger monthly payment for the rest of his life. If you work out the mathematics, the discounting for such a long period of time will imply that you pay mere pennies on the dollar. You will thus never outlive your retirement resources.

Comparing Annuity Payouts

Figure 2.1 on the next page will give you an indication of annuity payout levels during the last 15 years (1985–2000) for men and women at age 65, based on a $100,000 RRSP. This is a payment-certain (PC) annuity. If the person dies within 10 years of buying the annuity, his or her heirs (spouse and children) are guaranteed to continue to receive the same flow of income for 10 years. But if he or she dies after Year 10, the payments cease at death. In theory, you can select any PC period from zero to 30 years. But the longer the period, the less monthly income you will receive.

As you can see, the payout per $100,000 has been declining, roughly in line with the reduction in interest rates during this same period. You can also see that males get more than females, reflecting their shorter life expectancy.

Remember, when you purchase a life annuity, it is nonreversible, so the credit rating of the company selling you the policy is extremely important. As we discuss in detail in Chapter 7, all firms face some chance of insolvency. You may therefore not be surprised to learn that companies with better (higher or healthier) credit ratings tend to be a bit more conservative in terms of what they pay. Figure 2.2 on the next page illustrates this tendency.

Figure 2.2 illustrates the relationship between credit rating and the income that companies are willing to pay in the form of life annuities. Notice, for example, that Great-West Life tends

Figure 2.1

Annuity Payouts at Age 65

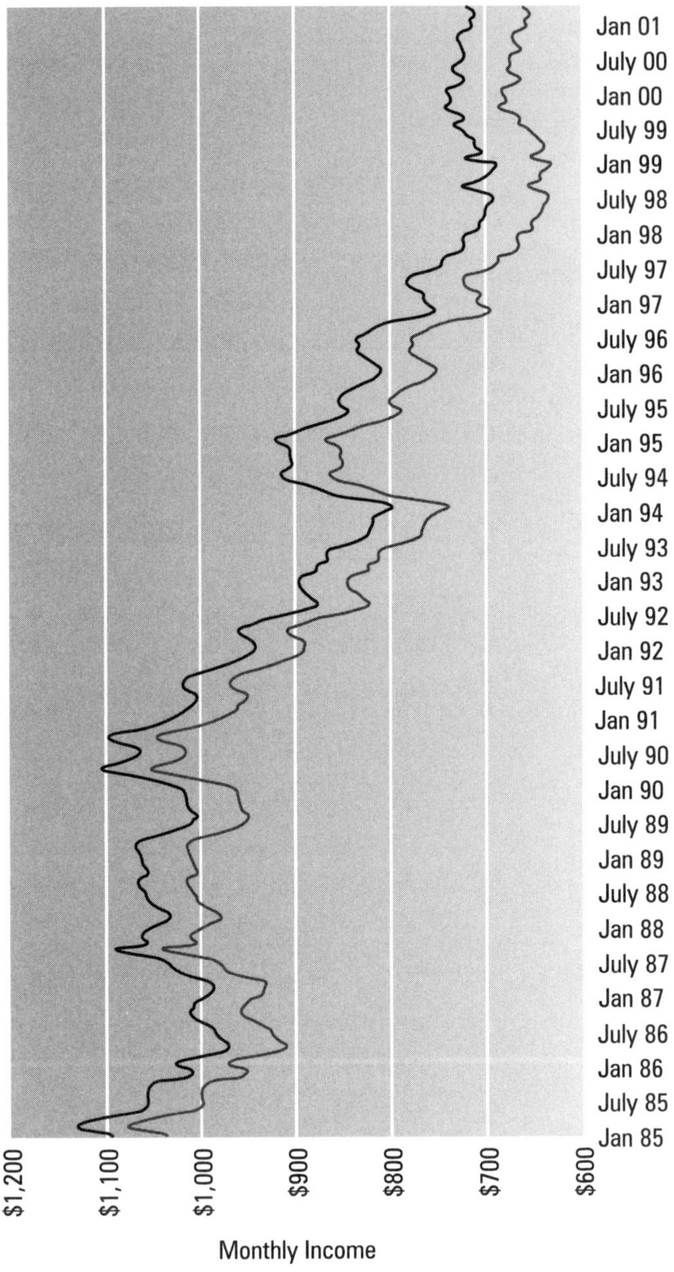

to pay less than average, compared to Royal & SunAlliance or Manulife, but Great-West's credit rating is higher, which means it is justified in being more cautious and not paying too much. We, as consumers, should be willing to accept lower payments in exchange for greater security that the company will still be around in 20 or 30 years.

Relationship Between Credit Rating and Average Annuity Payouts

Figure 2.2

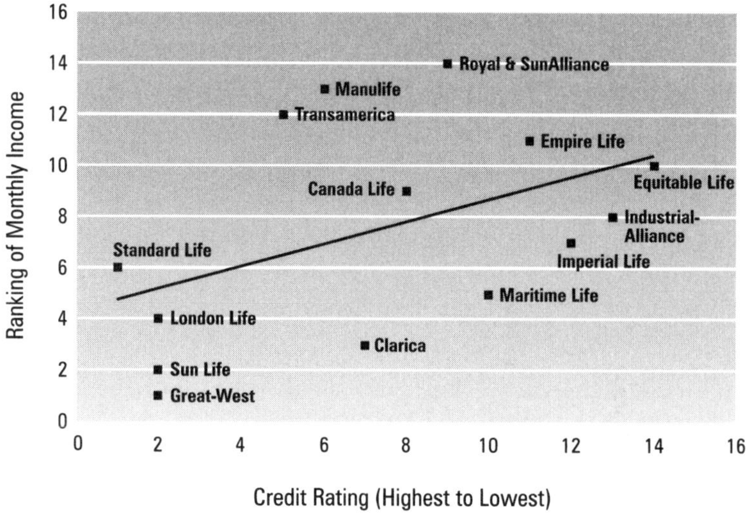

Some Additional Tax Advantages

It doesn't take a Ph.D. in finance to know that one minus one is precisely zero. If you add something and then take it away, you should end up exactly where you started. In practice, however, if you attempt to undo things, you may be left with less than zero. Did you ever buy a stock, only to regret it a few seconds later? By the time you reversed the transaction by selling the stock, you probably lost money on commissions and the bid/ask spread.

But this pattern has at least one notable exception. When you do and undo a particular type of insurance policy, you will end up financially better off than where you started. Moreover, consciously pursuing this strategy provides an excellent investment opportunity, generating pre-tax returns of up to 11% and perhaps even higher, with absolutely no risk whatsoever. Sounds like the proverbial free lunch? Well, it's more like a free dinner, served up by the Canada Income Tax Act. We call it the *mortality swap*, although insurance advisers like to refer to it as a back-to-back insurance and annuity contract.[2]

We'll describe how it works, but first, a bit of background. In theory, life insurance companies provide two basic services — life insurance and life annuities — that are symmetric opposites of each other. The basic principle of life insurance is that, in exchange for small monthly payments, the insurance company guarantees a large benefit upon your death. Life annuities, on the other hand, essentially provide protection against living too long; in exchange for one large payment now, the insurance company guarantees a small but steady monthly benefit until your demise. Traditionally, life insurance is acquired early in the human life cycle to protect your loved ones, while annuities are purchased during the "golden years" to protect yourself.

Now here is where things get interesting. Consider the idea of investing $100,000 to buy a life annuity and then using the monthly benefits to fund a life insurance policy with a $100,000 death benefit. Pointless? Taking expenses, commissions, and fees into account, you might think you'd be burning money.

However, interestingly enough, it turns out that one minus one is more than zero. If you buy a life annuity and then "reverse" it

2 See Narat Charupat and Moshe A. Milevsky, "Mortality Swaps and Tax Arbitrage in the Canadian Insurance and Annuity Market," *Journal of Risk and Insurance* 68:2 (2001), 102–35.

with life insurance, you will end up with a better return (after taxes) than if you had bought a generic coupon-bearing bond. In other words, it's a pretty sound investment. The exact reason is somewhat complicated — and please don't try this at home without parental supervision — but the key lies in the way that qualified life insurance and life annuities are taxed. They both have more lenient tax treatment — you either pay less or you pay it later — which means that they are preferable to other fixed-income investments, such as provincial and federal bonds.

Table 2.3 should give you a feel for the numbers, although exact prices can change from day to day. It shows the approximate annual insurance premiums and annuity payments on a $100,000 policy for a woman.

Table 2.3
Mortality Swap on a $100,000 Policy

Age of Female Buying Mortality Swap	Annual Life Insurance Premium	Annual Life Annuity Benefits (50% Marginal Bracket)	Equivalent Pre-tax Return (50% Marginal Bracket)
65	$ 2,566	$ 8,112	8.0%
70	3,566	9,357	8.4
75	4,919	10,812	9.1
80	6,654	13,162	10.9

For example, a 65-year-old female with $100,000 to invest would receive $8,112 per year from a life annuity in monthly instalments for the rest of her natural life. Of this $8,112, a relatively small portion, $3,137 — and this is the key — would be taxable. At a 50% marginal tax bracket, this would leave our 65-year-old with a net annuity cash flow of $6,543.50 ($8,112 – [0.5 x $3,137]) per year after taxes had been paid. Next, deduct the insurance premiums on a $100,000 policy, and she is left with

$3,977 ($6,543 – $2,566). Remember, all the taxes have been paid and the $3,977 is hers to keep. For an investment to generate the same after-tax cash flow, the woman would have to earn 8% on her $100,000 (this is why the table states that her equivalent pre-tax return is 8%). The same strategy for a 75-year-old female would yield an equivalent pre-tax return of 9.1%. These numbers are much higher than comparable bond yields.

The mortality swap works even better (you will earn a higher return) if the insurance and annuity you buy are "joint and last survivor" with your spouse. This means that payments and benefits will continue until the surviving spouse's demise. In addition, borrowing money to buy the life annuity and then buying life insurance will lead to even higher returns on investment, because leverage always magnifies investment gains. As you can see, the older you are, the larger your investment return, which is why we call this a free dinner instead of lunch!

Some caveats are in order, though. For this to work, you have to be healthy enough to qualify for the life insurance coverage. Also, you should try to buy the life annuity and the life insurance from two separate companies (separate underwriting, in insurance jargon). Otherwise, the Canada Customs and Revenue Agency (CCRA) won't wink at this stratagem — and they'll take back your free dinner.

Summary Points

- While age 85 is the typical assumed life expectancy, evidence suggests that over 50% of females and over 40% of males will still be alive at 85. For married couples, in over 70% of cases at least one of them will still be alive at 85. Retirement income planning must take this longevity risk into account. If you annuitize, you are transferring the longevity risk to an insurance company. If you decide not to annuitize, you are retaining the longevity risk.

- Purchasing a life annuity involves giving a non-refundable lump sum of money to an insurance company in exchange for a monthly or quarterly income stream. In fixed-term annuities, the income ends after a predetermined or fixed period. With purely life-contingent annuity products, the income ends upon the death of the annuitant or, in some cases, upon the surviving spouse's death. Consumers buy life annuities because they are afraid of living too long, so they add income to support the extra years of life.
- Insurance companies can guarantee annuity payments because they sell policies to many people in the same risk category. By doing so, an insurance company is able to hedge the risks by diversifying. While the company does not know how long each customer will live, it is able to estimate the profile of a large group of customers.
- The ideal longevity insurance product includes a plain fixed immediate annuity; provides the ability to protect a dependant or spouse; allows you to pick a suitable asset mix; permits rebalancing, deferment, liquidity, and the ability to lock in rates; and allows you to compute easily and transparently exactly how much your accumulation will buy in the immediate annuity market.
- In a "mortality swap," an individual invests in a life annuity and then uses the monthly benefits to fund a life insurance policy with a death benefit equivalent to the initial investment. By doing so, the individual ends up with a better return after taxes than from a generic coupon-bearing bond.

How to Sound Intelligent

Questions to Ask When Purchasing Longevity Insurance

- Should I transfer my longevity risk to an insurance company by purchasing longevity insurance, or am I willing to retain the risk myself?

- Should I obtain a fixed immediate annuity or a variable immediate annuity? Which asset mix is suitable for me?
- Does the longevity insurance give me the ability to select survivorship and certainty periods to protect my spouse and dependants?
- Does the product allow me to rebalance the asset mix between fixed and variable products during the payout phase?
- Should I defer the purchase of an immediate annuity until I am older?
- Can I lock in mortality and interest rates on the immediate annuity upon retirement?
- Am I able to easily and transparently compute exactly how much my accumulation will buy in the immediate annuity market?
- Can I liquidate the immediate annuity contract during the payment-certain period?
- Have I considered setting up a mortality swap?

3

Health Insurance and Travel Insurance

For those who believe that insurance is a less than fascinating topic, consider this: The vast majority of Canadians consider Canada's health care system, which is characterized by publicly funded health insurance, as an important part of being Canadian. According to a *Maclean's*/CBC poll conducted in 1999, no less than 79% of Canadians surveyed considered the Canadian health care system "an important part of what makes us Canadian."[3] The poll suggests, in fact, that many of these respondents consider the health care system to be as important to our national identity as Canada's climate and geography, its flag, and the achievements of prominent Canadians.

But Canada's public health insurance, also known as Medicare, does not provide truly complete coverage. As anyone who has ever had a cavity filled or who has fallen ill outside of Canada is aware, the coverage provided is extremely limited. To fill the gap between health care needs and public health

3 B. Wallace, "What Makes a Canadian?" *Maclean's* (December 20, 1999), 32–36.

insurance, Canadians turn to private health insurance products. In this chapter we explore health insurance and a related topic, travel insurance. Let's begin by reviewing the health care system in Canada, and the advantages and disadvantages associated with public health insurance.

Public Health Insurance in Canada

Public health insurance has been available in Canada — in different forms and in different jurisdictions — for over 50 years. The first province to establish universal hospital insurance was Saskatchewan, in 1947. Ten years later, Parliament passed the Hospital Insurance and Diagnostic Act, which required the federal government to share in the funding of hospital insurance. By 1961 all jurisdictions were providing insurance for hospital care.

The next year, the cycle of legislation began again. In 1962 Saskatchewan established insurance for visits to a physician. Six years later, the Medical Care Act required the federal government to share in the funding of medical care. By 1972, visits to physicians were publicly insured in all jurisdictions.

In 1984, because of concerns about physicians extra-billing and hospital user fees, Parliament unanimously passed the Canada Health Act, which remains in effect today. While the provinces and territories are constitutionally responsible for the administration and delivery of health care, the federal government transfers funds to those jurisdictions under a mechanism known as the Canada Health and Social Transfer. The Canada Health Act specifies criteria and conditions that jurisdictions must satisfy in order to receive federal transfers of cash to fund health care. Hence, while the province or territory can choose to provide health services beyond the Canada Health Act, if it fails to meet the conditions and criteria specified in the act, particularly with regard to user charges and extra-billing, it faces deductions from its transfer payments.

The principal criteria specified in the Canada Health Act are public administration, comprehensiveness, universality, portability, and accessibility. The public administration criterion requires that health care insurance be provided on a non-profit basis and be accountable to the provincial or territorial government. The comprehensiveness criterion specifies that the health insurance plan must insure "all" health services. The universality criterion specifies that all insured residents be entitled to health services. The portability criterion specifies that the home province or territory must continue to provide coverage for residents who are temporarily absent from the province, or during a waiting period of up to three months after they have moved out of the jurisdiction.

The accessibility criterion specifies that coverage cannot be dependent on user fees, health, or age. However, the accessibility criterion includes a "where and as available" rule, which means that you have to accept the services where they are available and as they are available. As well, the accessibility criterion requires the province or territory to compensate health care providers and hospitals.

The two conditions specified in the Canada Health Act are the information condition and the recognition condition. The information condition requires the jurisdiction to provide information about the services provided to the federal minister of health. The recognition condition requires the jurisdiction to publicize the fact that it has received federal contributions.

The Canada Health Act specifies coverage for medically necessary hospital services, physician services, and surgical dental services. As well, some extended health care services are specified, such as certain aspects of long-term residential care, home care, and ambulatory care. As mentioned earlier, the province or territory may also choose to provide services beyond the Canada Health Act. Hence, the coverage provided in each jurisdiction may differ.

Exactly what is — and what is not — covered by public health insurance? Table 3.1 provides a general overview. As is apparent from the table, most health care services are not fully financed publicly, and many receive no public funding at all.

Table 3.1
Financing of Health Care Services in Canada

Health Care Service	Source of Financing
Public health	Primarily public
Hospital services	Primarily public
Services to status Indians and Inuit	Primarily public
Physician services	Primarily public
Home care	Mixed
Rehabilitation services	Mixed
Residential long-term care	Mixed
Ambulances	Mixed
Prescription drugs	Mixed
Dental and optometry services	Primarily private
Non-prescription drugs	Primarily private
Other health care professionals	Primarily private
Alternative medicine	Primarily private

Source: Canadian Institute for Health Information, *Health Care in Canada* (Ottawa: Canadian Institute for Health Information, 2000), 17.

As a specific example, let's explore the comprehensiveness and portability — two of the criteria listed earlier — of coverage provided in Ontario, Canada's largest province. Of course, the details will evolve over time as governments change and legislation is passed. And, while coverage is generally similar across jurisdictions, there are numerous differences worthy of note. For example, some jurisdictions provide more extensive coverage for prescription drugs than others. For details regarding your jurisdiction, contact your provincial or territorial government.

The Ontario Example: Comprehensiveness

Services covered by public health insurance in Ontario can be categorized in terms of physician services, surgical dental services, inpatient hospital services, outpatient services, and other services. Of these services, some are insured, but many are not.

For example, insured physician services include medical examinations and tests, diagnosis and treatment of medical disabilities and conditions, and surgical procedures. Insured surgical dental services include repair of traumatic injuries and surgical incisions. Insured inpatient hospital services include accommodation and meals at the standard ward level and use of operating rooms. Insured outpatient services include laboratory, radiological, and other diagnostic procedures and radiotherapy. Examples of other services provided include mental health services and residential care services.

The above are examples of the many health services insured, most of which are at least vaguely familiar to Canadians. Of more relevance to this chapter are those health services that are not publicly insured and for which private insurance may enable one to get protection. Many hospital services are not covered. For example, public health insurance will not provide preferred accommodation in a hospital unless prescribed by a physician. Other "bells and whistles" associated with a hospital stay are also not covered, including use of a telephone or television and private-duty nursing. Further, take-home medication and in-province hospital visits solely for the administration of drugs are not insured, with some exceptions.

Numerous physician services are not covered as well, including those in the list that follows:[4]

- services that are not medically necessary
- travelling to visit an insured person outside the area of practice
- toll charges for long-distance telephone calls
- preparation or provision of a drug, antigen, antiserum, or other substance
- advice given by telephone at the request of the insured person or the person's representative
- interviews or case conferences
- preparation and transfer of records at the insured person's request
- services received wholly or partly for the production or completion of a document or the transmission of information, in specified circumstances
- production or completion of a document or the transmission of information to any person other than the insured person, in specified circumstances
- provision of a prescription when no concomitant insured service is rendered
- cosmetic surgery
- acupuncture procedures
- psychological testing
- group screening programs
- research and survey programs

(This list is not exhaustive and may be subject to exceptions.)

Finally, many other health-related services, such as provision of prescription drugs, eyewear, and dental services, are also not covered under public health insurance.

4 Source: *Canada Health Act Annual Report* (Ottawa: Health Canada, 1999–2000).

The Ontario Example: Portability

What coverage does public health insurance provide if a resident of Ontario temporarily travels outside the province? Consider a situation in which a resident of Ontario works or travels out of province, but still within Canada, without establishing residency. In that case, the Interprovincial Agreement on Eligibility and Portability stipulates that the resident can use his or her Ontario health card to receive health services. Ontario provides this coverage for 12 months, or longer if the resident or a family member is studying in another Canadian jurisdiction.

If an Ontario resident travels outside of Canada, health insurance coverage may be provided for an extended absence longer than 212 days, typically following submission of a document explaining the absence. But to qualify, the resident must have been in Ontario for at least 153 days in each of the two years prior to departure. Table 3.2 specifies the health insurance coverage provided for different extended absences, which also applies to family members of the primary applicant.

Table 3.2

Approved Out-of-Country Extended Absences from Ontario

Reason	**Coverage**
Study	Duration of a full-time academic program (unlimited)
Work	Five-year terms
Missionary work	Duration of missionary activities (unlimited)
Vacation or other	Up to two years in a lifetime

Source: *Canada Health Act Annual Report* (Ottawa: Health Canada, 1999–2000).

Should an Ontario resident require out-of-country elective surgery, prior approval must be received. If the treatment is unavailable in Ontario, or if life or irreversible tissue damage is threatened, the patient is entitled to full funding. In most cases, no prior approval is required within Canada.

What if you have moved to Ontario from another jurisdiction? Canadians previously insured in another Canadian jurisdiction are covered beginning the first day of the third month of residing in Ontario. Canadians returning from a foreign country are covered after three months of residence in Ontario.

Superficially, our Ontario example suggests that there is no need for travel insurance — after all, coverage is available when travelling out of province, whether inside or outside Canada! However, as we will discuss later on in this chapter, the out-of-country protection provided by public health insurance is insufficient. One reason is that, while coverage is provided, there are specified maximum dollar limits to the coverage. Some of those limits may be well below the cost of the services you would require in an emergency. This is particularly true in the United States, where hospital expenses can be high.

How Much of Heath Care Is Publicly Funded?

As we demonstrate above, while public health coverage is extensive, numerous health services are not covered. Evidence suggests that the amount Canadians spend on private insurance, both on a per capita basis and as a percentage of total spending, is significant. To demonstrate, let's begin by taking a snapshot of per capita health expenditure in Canada from 1975 through 2000 by source of financing, in current dollars (1999 and 2000 values are forecasts).

Figure 3.1 indicates that per capita expenditure on health has increased dramatically over the 25-year period, with the exception of limited growth in the early to mid 1990s that fol-

Per Capita Canadian Health Expenditure, 1975–2000

Figure 3.1

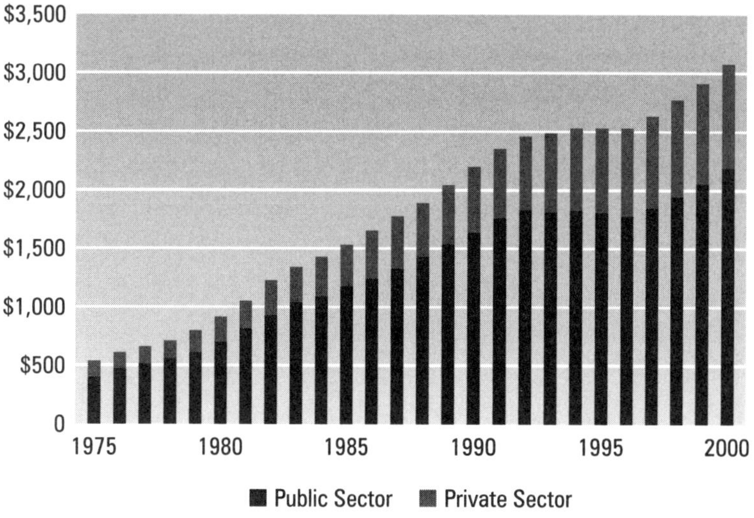

Source: Canadian Institute for Health Information, 2000.

lowed funding cuts. The historical evidence also suggests that private sector spending in health care has grown at a faster rate than public sector spending.

Total health expenditure as a percentage of the GDP (gross domestic product, the total value of goods and services produced in the economy) grew from 7% in 1975 to a high of 10% in 1992.[5] Health expenditure as a percentage of GDP has declined somewhat since then, but remains above 9%.

What percentage of this spending is publicly financed, and what percentage is privately financed? Private sector expenditure grew from 23.8% of total health spending in 1975 to a projected 29.5% in 1999.[6] However, private sector expenditure as a percentage of total health expenditure varies widely from

5 Canadian Institute for Health Information, 2000.

6 Ibid.

jurisdiction to jurisdiction. Figure 3.3 presents forecasted private expenditure as a percentage of total expenditure for all Canadian jurisdictions in 1999. Ontario has the highest private sector expenditure, at 34%, while the Northwest Territories and Nunavut have the lowest, at 8%.

Private Sector Health Care Spending in Canada, 1999

Figure 3.2

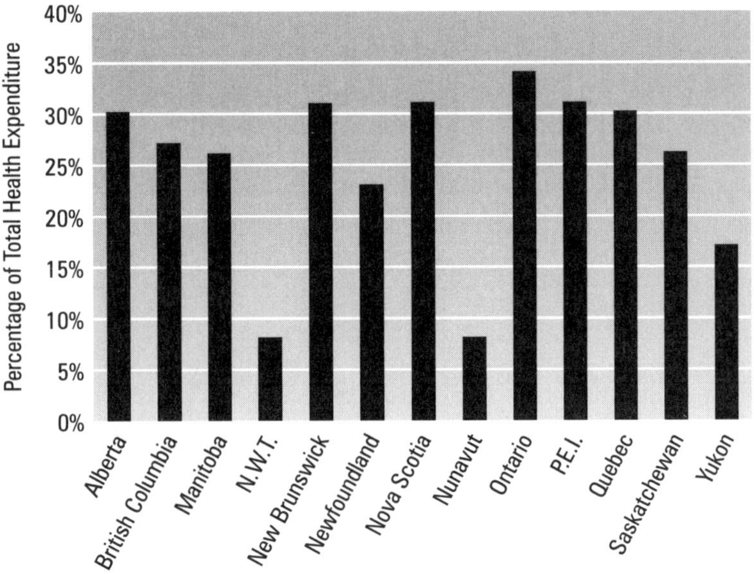

Source: Canadian Institute for Health Information, *Health Care in Canada* (Ottawa: Canadian Institute for Health Information, 2000), 19.

The extent to which individuals are covered by private health insurance is a function of social standing. Evidence suggests that those with the lowest incomes or limited education are the least likely to have private health insurance coverage. This is not surprising, as private health insurance is expensive, and it is often provided through work. Table 3.3 shows a breakdown of the percentage of Canadians holding dental care insurance, corrective eyewear insurance, and prescription drug insurance, by income and education level.

Table 3.3
Canadians with Private Health Insurance

	Dental Care	Corrective Eyewear	Prescription Drugs
Education			
Less than high school	48%	45%	71%
High school	55	52	72
College	59	51	75
University	66	60	80
Income			
Lowest income	30%	29%	58%
Lower middle income	41	37	66
Upper middle income	65	59	80
Highest income	79	70	87
Not stated	50	46	73

Source: National Population Health Survey, Statistics Canada (Ottawa: Canadian Institute for Health Information, 2000), 21.

As Table 3.3 indicates, people with a university education hold each type of coverage in greater percentages than any other education level. A similar result is found for those in the highest income bracket. Fewer than half of those with less than a high school education and fewer than a third of those in the lowest income bracket have dental care or corrective eyewear coverage. At the same time, much higher percentages of each hold prescription drug coverage. Interestingly, prescription drug coverage is more extensively reported than the other two types of coverage for all social classes. This suggests that prescription drug coverage is either less expensive than the other types of coverage, or of much greater importance to Canadians.

Advantages and Disadvantages of Public Health Insurance

The survey cited at the beginning of this chapter (about the importance of the health care system to Canadians' identity) suggests that it might be unpatriotic to explore public health insurance in Canada too meticulously. However, people are increasingly questioning the quality of the existing health care system. A recent poll asked Canadians to grade "the overall quality of the health care services available to you and your family," as either A, B, C, or F.[7] On average, those polled conferred a rating of B, and rated government performance in dealing with health care much lower.

To consider the advantages and disadvantages of public health insurance, let's look at the characteristics of the plan as we would for any other insurance product. We characterize public health insurance as a *tax-revenue subsidized, freely available, government-controlled, nondiscriminatory, and noncancellable group insurance plan with no deductibles or market competition.* In our view, while public health insurance may be an important component of our Canadian identity, it is also just another insurance plan, and should be evaluated as such. To do so, let's consider the characteristics of public health insurance in detail.

Tax-Subsidized and Freely Available Services

An important characteristic of public health insurance in Canada is that it is tax-subsidized and freely available to all, regardless of economic standing. This is advantageous, many argue, as no one has to choose between health services and putting food on the table. A related advantage is that it allows society to avoid scenarios in which people fail to obtain protection against

7 Ipsos-Reid poll conducted for the Canadian Medical Association, in *National Report Card 2001* (Canadian Medical Association, July 2001).

the financial burden associated with health needs, under the mistaken impression that they will never get seriously ill.

Homogeneous Group Plan

Another characteristic of public health insurance is that it is a group plan, offering the same, homogeneous package of health services to all Canadians, no more and no less. Some consider the homogeneity to be an advantage. An argument often cited by certain segments of the political spectrum is that the homogeneity allows the country to avoid an "inequitable" two-tiered system in which some get better health services than others. A two-tiered system is perceived as inequitable because some people could receive better health services simply because they are able — and willing — to pay for them. Some argue also that a two-tiered system would result in high-quality health care professionals choosing to provide services only to the upper tier because of the added financial incentive.

Others argue that the homogeneity has economic advantages. In economic terms, health care is an "experience good" — a good that must be experienced before you can determine its worth. After all, few individuals know whether they really need the treatments recommended by their health professionals. To be on the safe side, their tendency is to accept the advice and proceed with the treatment in spite of not knowing its usefulness. This results in overuse of health services. However, Canada's homogeneous public health insurance plan sets limits on the types and extent of health services one can receive, so opportunities to overuse health services are restricted. Another economic advantage is that, because it is a group plan, public health insurance has purchasing power that can enable some services to be provided at a discount.

But others consider the homogeneity associated with public

health insurance to be a disadvantage. After all, we have the freedom to choose the dental services we want and the type of housing we live in. Why shouldn't we have the freedom to choose to spend more on health? As well, some argue, the health care system is already two-tiered in many ways. For example, workplace safety and compensation boards block-purchase time for MRI scans, effectively resulting in queue-jumping.[8] As well, those who can afford it can travel to the United States for superior health care service. When asked how he would change the Canada Health Act, Arnold Aberman, then dean of the University of Toronto medical school, didn't pull any punches when he answered, "Decriminalize medical acts between consenting adults and allow patients to purchase more medical care than the government provides."[9]

Interestingly, this argument has some support among Canadians. A recent survey found an even split — 33% agreeing and 33% disagreeing — in response to the statement "A good way to sustain the healthcare system over the long run is to start having the public pay for some services."[10] But another survey found that 52% of Canadians disagreed with the statement "Individuals should be allowed to pay extra to get quicker access to health care services," while 36% agreed.[11] Not surprisingly, those most able to afford to pay extra — the "upper class" — were more supportive of the idea, with 52% agreeing and 40% disagreeing. Among those least able to afford to pay extra — "the poor" — 26% agreed with the statement, while 66% disagreed.

8 C. D. Naylor, "Health Care in Canada: Incrementalism Under Financial Distress," *Health Affairs* (May/June, 1999).
9 "Opening Up the Canada Health Act: Can Its Principles Remain Intact?" *Health Policy Forum* (June/July 1998).
10 Ipsos-Reid poll conducted for the Canadian Medical Association, in *National Report Card 2001*, (Canadian Medical Association, July 2001).
11 EKOS Research Associates Inc. poll cited in J. Geddes, "No Two-tier Health Care?" *Maclean's* (July 9, 2001).

Lack of Competition

Another characteristic of public health insurance is that it is non-competitive. Two advantages of lack of competition are that there is no need to spend funds on marketing efforts such as advertising and sales commissions, and no need to provide investors with a return on their money. However, the lack of market competition is disadvantageous as well. Market competition forces insurance providers to keep costs low and quality high in order to attract customers. Competition effectively increases efficiency and gives consumers a chance to "vote" in favour of one provider or another by obtaining insurance through them.

Government Control

Another characteristic of public health insurance is that it is government controlled. An advantage of government control is that it eliminates many of the frictions one may face when dealing with a private insurance company. As we discuss extensively in Chapter 7, the quality of an insurance policy arises from more than the sum of the details specified in its fine print. Consumers must consider whether the insurance company will satisfy claims as promised, whether it will become insolvent before the insured event, and whether the intermediary is honestly representing the consumer's best interests, among many other considerations. With a government-controlled system, many, if not all of these frictions are eliminated. For example, since public health insurance is not "sold," there is no concern that an agent or broker will misrepresent the policy for the purpose of making a quick buck.

Interestingly, a recent poll found that 30% agreed while 37% disagreed when presented with the statement "A good way to sustain the health care system over the long run is to allow the private sector to manage it, because it is more efficient than governments."[12] While not an overwhelming rejection of private sector management, it does suggest that Canadians have misgivings about placing health care management in private hands.

As an example of how insurance companies can be overly inflexible, consider the following study from the United States, where basic health care is, for the most part, privately insured.[13] The study surveyed 1,124 randomly chosen practising physicians in 1998, asking them whether they used one of the following tactics, "sometimes" or more often, to help their patients secure coverage for needed care: exaggerating the severity of the patient's condition, changing the patient's billing diagnosis, and/or reporting signs or symptoms that the patient did not have. The survey found that 39% of the physicians reported using at least one tactic. While these actions may be fraudulent (see Chapter 8), the high proportion of doctors willing to stretch the truth for their patients suggests that insurance companies may be overly strict about restrictions in the U.S. health care insurance system.

Lack of Deductibles

Another characteristic of public health insurance is that there are no deductibles. Indeed, an important feature of the Canada Health Act is its rejection of user charges and extra-billing. But, as we discuss briefly in Chapter 1 and throughout this book, there are advantages associated with deductibles.

Generally speaking, the higher the deductible, the lower the cost of insurance, because deductibles eliminate numerous

12 Ipsos-Reid poll conducted for the Canadian Medical Association, in *National Report Card 2001* (Canadian Medical Association, July 2001).

13 M. K. Wynia, D. S. Cummins, J. B. VanGeest, and I. B. Wilson, "Physician Manipulation of Reimbursement Rules for Patients: Between a Rock and a Hard Place," *Journal of the American Medical Association* 283:14 (2000), 1858.

small claims. Since public health insurance has no deductibles, Canadians access health care services freely. But the purpose of health insurance should be to minimize the financial burden of health care, not to motivate people to use services unnecessarily — services that they would not use if they had to pay for a portion. Hence, even a small deductible could eliminate exploitation of the health system for services that are not really necessary, and free up resources for more important needs. Recognition that the health care system is misused in Canada is widespread; a recent poll found that 61% of Canadians believe that "many people misuse the health-care system."[14]

Lack of Discrimination

Another characteristic of public health insurance is that it is non-discriminatory. This means that everyone within the same tax bracket pays the same amount for public health insurance, regardless of health status or personal habits. An individual who smokes cigarettes and who trains lions for a living pays the same amount for health insurance as a non-smoker who works in an office and jogs 10 kilometres per day. As a result, public health insurance is underpriced for those with a high probability and magnitude of health problems, while overpriced for those in good health, who are associated with low probability and magnitude of health problems.

Contrast this non-discriminatory characteristic of public health insurance with private insurance. For example, the lion trainer who smokes would have a difficult time finding a private insurance company willing to provide life insurance — and if a provider were found, the policy would be very costly in order to reflect the risks involved.

14 Ipsos-Reid poll conducted for the Canadian Medical Association, in *National Report Card 2001* (Canadian Medical Association, July 2001).

Protection from Cancellation

As discussed in Chapter 1 and elsewhere in this book, *moral hazard* occurs in situations when an individual behaves recklessly, knowing that the insurance provider can't observe the behaviour and that he or she will not incur the cost of that behaviour. An implicit feature of public health insurance is that it cannot be cancelled. Regardless of how many times a person accesses the system because of reckless behaviour, the "policy" can't be cancelled and the individual can continue to access service. Consider behaviour that some might call reckless (though others may vehemently disagree): biking without a helmet. The costs of biking without a helmet include increased probability of personal injury or death. One can reasonably argue that at least some individuals who currently bike without a helmet would wear a helmet if public health insurance were cancellable. But public health insurance continues to provide services indiscriminately to those who bike without helmets, regardless of the number of accidents in which they are involved. Deductibles play a similar role in reducing moral hazard: The higher the direct cost to an individual, the less likely the individual is to engage in reckless behaviour.

How Does Private Health Insurance Work?

As we've demonstrated extensively, while public health insurance is available in Canada, it does not finance all health services. Many health services are either financed through primarily private sources, or receive a mixture of private and public financing. To obtain protection for those services not covered by public health insurance, people must obtain private health insurance, either through group plans or on an individual basis. Private health insurance provides coverage for financially burdensome, non-routine events, such as high drug costs for a critical illness. But it also provides health services that are required on a routine basis, in contrast to other types of insurance — such as disability or property insurance — that provide protection exclusively for non-routine insurable events.

Many of the services for which private health insurance provides coverage are not beyond the ability of a typical Canadian household to afford. But, while each health service may not be financially burdensome on its own, the accumulated costs of these health services can be onerous.

If you are employed by a large enough business, you very likely receive health insurance as part of a group plan. A group plan will typically include a package of benefits that may comprise some or all of the following:

- life insurance (discussed in Chapter 1)
- accidental death and dismemberment insurance
- health insurance
- dental insurance
- short-term disability insurance (discussed in Chapter 4)
- long-term disability insurance (discussed in Chapter 4)
- critical illness insurance (discussed in Chapter 4)
- travel insurance (to be discussed in more detail in this chapter)

The health care benefits offered by a group plan can also include prescription drugs, hospital care, medical services and equipment, nursing services, emergency travel assistance, and corrective eyewear. As well, they may include paramedical services (for example, those provided by speech therapists and podiatrists) and psychosocial interventions (for example, assistance from psychologists and social workers to solve personal problems such as stress or drug abuse).

Depending on the plan, dental insurance can include preventive, basic, restorative, and orthodontic treatments. Preventive treatment may include x-rays, oral examinations, laboratory tests, and space maintainers. Basic treatment may include periodontic and endodontic services, treatments for dentures, oral surgery, and anesthesia. Restorative treatments may include crowns, prosthodontic appliances, and denture repair. Orthodontic treatments may include observations and adjustments, fixed or cemented appliances, and appliances to control harmful oral habits. The above are just examples; many other treatments may be covered as well.

Group plans are advantageous because their purchasing power enables the group to obtain insurance at a discount. However, group plans are typically homogeneous, and they only last as long as you are part of the group — you can't take your group plan with you if you quit your job. If your group plan is too limited, you may wish to obtain individual private health insurance to supplement the health insurance provided by the group plan.

If your employer does not provide health insurance, or if you are self-employed, you can purchase private health insurance on an individual basis. The coverage offered is quite flexible. As one would expect, the higher the premium you are willing to pay, the more extensive the coverage will be. To demonstrate the relationship between premium and coverage, consider the individual private health insurance offered by Blue Cross in Quebec. Table 3.4 details some alternative combinations of health benefits, with their associated premiums, under Blue Cross's Health Plus plan. We assume throughout that the coverage is for a family in which the oldest person receiving coverage is a 40-year-old male. Further, assume that the premiums are paid monthly.

Table 3.4
Combinations of Health Benefits and Associated Premiums
(Blue Cross Health Plus Plan, August, 2001)

Coverage Provided	Monthly Premium
Accident and sickness plus travel insurance	$81.01
Above coverage plus prescription drugs	$107.42
All above coverage plus dental care	$171.16
All above coverage plus regular home health care	$183.36
All above coverage plus $50 daily compensation while in hospital	$205.56

As we see from Table 3.4, premiums begin at $81.01 for the base plan, which consists of accident and sickness plus travel insurance coverage. But the monthly premiums increase as each option is added, reaching $205.56 for a plan consisting of the base plan plus coverage for prescription drugs, dental care, regular home health care, and $50 daily compensation while in hospital. The plans specified in Table 3.4 are only a few of the many combinations possible. For example, you may wish to forgo prescription drug coverage and dental care, creating instead a package consisting of the base plan plus home health care and daily compensation. Health insurance packages are also available for people over 55 to provide protection for their specific health concerns.

While insurance companies will provide insurance for health services that may be required on a routine basis, they will typically not provide insurance for a pre-existing condition. For example, people with HIV are unlikely to be able to find an insurance provider willing to provide protection, because of the high costs associated with treating that condition. Insurance may be available in the case of some pre-existing conditions, such as pregnancy, but coverage will be excluded for health services specifically associated with that condition. Another way that insurance companies limit the risk associated with a pre-existing condition is by setting limits on the amount of coverage.

How Does Travel Insurance Work?

As we discussed earlier, one of the criteria specified by the Canada Health Act is portability. This criterion specifies that the home province or territory must continue to provide coverage for residents temporarily absent from the province, or during a waiting period of up to three months when they have moved out of the jurisdiction.

But, as we saw from the example of Ontario, there are limitations as to how provinces apply the portability criterion. Out-of-province health insurance is generally comprehensive within Canada because of accords such as the Interprovincial Agreement on Eligibility and Portability, though Quebec's participation in the agreement is limited. But once you leave Canada, your provincial or territorial insurance imposes upper limits on the extent of coverage, limits that may be insufficient should an emergency occur. For example, Ontario specifies a maximum $400 (Canadian) per diem limit for inpatient emergency hospital costs and a maximum $50 (Canadian) limit for outpatient health services. In some U.S. hospitals, however, daily expenses may be in the thousands of dollars.

Travel insurance is designed to overcome the gap between the coverage provided by public health insurance and the coverage actually required. As we saw earlier, some group plans include travel insurance. As well, you may have travel insurance through a premium (gold or platinum) credit card, though it may include conditions and limitations. If you don't have insurance through a group plan or a credit card, you may wish to purchase travel insurance individually.

The vast majority of Canadians are covered by travel insurance when they leave the country. One survey found that 80% of Canadians had some type of travel health insurance on their last leisure trip out of the country.[15] However, millions of Canadians continue to travel outside the country without private health insurance, although their number is declining. While 4,621,000 Canadians travelled outside the country without travel insurance in 1996, "only" 2,925,000 did so in 1999.[16] Not surprisingly, young travellers, who tend to feel invincible (those between the ages of 18 and 25) were the least likely to be covered.

What is covered by travel insurance? Unlike private health insurance, which covers many health services, including those that are routine and expected, travel insurance is meant to assist in dealing with emergencies associated with your trip. Hence, it may provide protection against some or all of the following emergencies: emergency hospital/medical costs, trip cancellation (before and after departure), emergency departure, lost baggage, flight accident, and accidental death and dismemberment.

As with all private insurance, the premiums are directly related to the options you choose. If you require $2,500 coverage for lost baggage rather than $500, for example, expect to pay higher premiums. Similarly, if you choose to have only hospital and medical coverage and a high deductible, expect to pay much less.

As with health insurance, most policies will exclude or limit coverage for pre-existing conditions. For example, if you've had a heart attack in the past six months, it's unlikely that you will be able to obtain coverage for heart-related ailments. And don't think you can travel into a war zone and still be covered by travel insurance. Injuries caused by war, as well as sports

15 Survey reported in D. Redekop, *Travel Health Insurance: Risk Takers on Decline* (Conference Board of Canada, March 1999).
16 Ibid.

injuries, suicide, and problems posed by substance abuse, may not be covered.

Travel insurance can be purchased on a trip-by-trip basis, for all trips taken over a summer, or even for all trips taken over an entire year. Coverage for longer periods can be important for travellers such as "snowbirds" — people (usually older) who travel to warmer climates in the winter — and business travellers. Note that travel insurance is intended to cover emergencies, and does not include elective surgery, other health services, or coverage of pre-existing conditions, all of which snowbirds may require. For this reason, a number of companies sell "insurance for snowbirds." Business travellers must also be careful to ensure that they are covered; never just assume that your company provides travel insurance coverage.

As the Ontario example described earlier suggests, extra care must be taken with extended absences from your province or territory. If you intend to take an extended absence and want to continue to qualify for public health insurance benefits, you may have to submit an explanatory document to your provincial or territorial government. Remaining qualified is crucial, as travel insurance is usually conditional on being eligible for public health insurance.

Summary Points

- An important part of our identity as Canadians, public health insurance is based on the Canada Health Act, which stipulates criteria and conditions that jurisdictions must satisfy in order to receive federal transfers of cash to fund health care. It includes five criteria and two conditions. The criteria are *public administration*, *comprehensiveness*, *universality*, *portability*, and *accessibility*. The conditions are *information* and *recognition*.
- The comprehensiveness and portability criteria suggest that

all health services, anywhere in the world, are covered by public health insurance. In practice, however, the coverage is limited. While public health, hospital, and physician services are primarily publicly financed, many other health needs, such as prescription drugs and dental services, may not be. Similarly, while out-of-country travel is covered by public health insurance, the coverage often falls well below the required amount. Private health insurance and travel insurance fill the gap between public health insurance and the required level of service.

- Per capita expenditure on health spending has increased dramatically over the past quarter-century, with the exception of limited growth in the early to mid 1990s because of funding cuts. Private sector spending in health care has grown at a faster rate than public sector spending, rising from 23.8% in 1975 to a projected 29.5% in 1999. But private sector spending in Canada varies widely from jurisdiction to jurisdiction. In addition, the extent of private health insurance coverage is a function of education and income.
- Public health insurance is a tax-revenue–subsidized, freely available, government-controlled, non-discriminatory, and uncancellable group insurance plan with no deductibles or market competition. As such, it has many advantages and disadvantages.
- Private health insurance provides coverage for financially burdensome, non-routine events. But it also provides health services that are required on a routine basis, in contrast to other types of insurance, such as disability or property insurance, that provide protection exclusively for non-routine insurable events. While each service covered by private health insurance may not be financially burdensome on its own, the accumulated costs of these health services can be onerous.

- Travel insurance is designed to overcome the gap between the coverage public health insurance provides and the travel coverage required. Travel insurance is meant to assist in dealing with emergencies associated with the trip. Millions of Canadians continue to travel outside the country without private health insurance, although their number is declining.

How to Sound Intelligent

Questions to Ask When Purchasing Private Health Insurance

- What is covered through the public health insurance offered in my province or territory, and what is not?
- Of those health services not covered by public health insurance, which ones are important for me?
- Do I have health insurance through a group plan at work or elsewhere?
- If I have a group plan, is the coverage sufficient for my needs?
- Exactly how much am I paying in monthly premiums for each option I choose to include in my health insurance package?
- Have I informed the insurance company about any pre-existing conditions?

Questions to Ask When Purchasing Travel Insurance

- What coverage is provided by my province or territory? Is the coverage sufficient?
- Have I submitted all required documentation to my provincial or territorial government?
- Do I have travel insurance through a group plan at work or a credit card? What is and what is not covered?
- Which options should I obtain when purchasing travel insurance?

- What are the maximum limits associated with the travel insurance?
- Should I purchase insurance on a trip-by-trip basis or for longer increments of time?
- Have I considered obtaining "insurance for snowbirds"?

4

Disability Insurance and Critical Illness Insurance

Are the financial implications of your being disabled worse for your family than the financial implications of your death? For a surprisingly large number of us, the answer is yes. But, while we are careful to purchase life insurance to provide for our families when we die, we often are not as careful to protect them should we become disabled. If you rely on your paycheque to pay the bills, this is a serious omission. Your ability to generate income in the future — your human capital — is at risk if you have a disability. While simply having a disability does not necessarily prevent you from working, many people with disabilities are unemployed or unable to join the labour force. As Table 4.1 suggests, one's ability to work is a function of the severity of the disability.

Using the data in Table 4.1, we calculate that in the year of the study, approximately 52% of adult Canadians with disabilities were either unemployed or not in the labour force. How many of these individuals were insured against disability before being disabled? An even more interesting question to think

Table 4.1
Status of Persons with Disabilities, 1991

Severity	Total Disabled Persons in Category	Employed	Unemployed	Not in Labour Force
Mild	54%	62.1%	8.8%	29.1%
Moderate	32	37.4	7.4	55.2
Severe	14	18.5	7.2	74.4

Source: Gail Fawcett, *Living with Disability in Canada: An Economic Portrait* (Ottawa: Human Resources and Development Canada, 1996), Table 2.5.

about when deciding whether to purchase disability or critical illness insurance is, *How many of those who were uninsured when they suffered their disability regret not purchasing protection beforehand?*

In this chapter we focus on two types of insurance that you can buy to support you and your family should you become disabled. The first type, disability insurance, provides monthly benefits if you are unable to work because of a disability. The second type, critical illness insurance, provides a lump-sum payment if you are diagnosed with a critical illness. What benefits does one receive from each type of insurance? Which one is most appropriate for you? How are disability and critical illness insurance related to health and life insurance? Before we consider these issues, however, let's begin by exploring why planning for a future disability is an essential part of insurance planning, however unlikely the possibility of future disability may seem to you today.

Why Are Disability Insurance and/or Critical Illness Insurance Important?

The need to protect oneself against a future disability is often overlooked. This is because of two common misperceptions people have about the future. The first misperception is "I'll never be disabled." As we demonstrate below, historical evidence suggests that for many of us this is simply not true. Even if you think you are as strong as an ox, remember that even an ox can get sick, and even an ox can be involved in an accident!

The second misperception is "The government will take care of it." This misperception is quite dangerous, because there is a degree of truth involved. Government programs, such as Employment Insurance (EI), the Canada Pension Plan (CPP), and Quebec Pension Plan (QPP), and provincial workers' compensation boards (WCB, WSIB) do provide benefits to some. But unless you are prepared to accept a steep decline in your standard of living — or happen to be independently wealthy — these sources of benefits are insufficient.

Let's consider each misperception in detail.

Misperception 1: "I'll never be disabled."

It's very difficult for many of us to imagine being disabled for any length of time. We may pride ourselves on never missing a day of work (or only calling in sick to go fishing!). We may have had surgery in the past — maybe a gall bladder removed — and returned to work within two weeks or less. These life experiences make us confident that we can overcome any future illnesses or accidents. However, historical, empirical evidence suggests that this belief is caused by hubris — exaggerated self-confidence — and does not reflect reality. Your likelihood of facing a disability in the future is much greater than you might expect. It is potentially depressing, but quite useful, to review some historical evidence. We are confident that these statistics will make you think twice about your future disability insurance needs.

Your likelihood of suffering a disability before the age of 65 is much greater than your likelihood of death. Here are some facts: A person aged 25 is 3.6 times more likely to suffer a disability that lasts 90 days or more before the age of 65 than to die before that age.[17] The ratio of probability of disability to probability of death decreases over time. People aged 35 are 2.2 times more likely to suffer a disability than to die before 65, while those aged 45 are 1.4 times more likely.

Cynics — or those with unlimited hubris — will immediately try to counter these arguments. "Sure, I have a higher probability of disability than death before the age of 65. But the probability of either event is pretty low! So why should I bother protecting myself?" This is a valid argument. After all, an event can be three times more likely without being very likely at all. Consider two lotteries: One gives a 1-in-300 million chance to win $100 million, while the other offers a 1-in-100 million chance of winning. We can accurately state that a ticket holder is three times more likely to win the second lottery than the first. But we wouldn't mortgage our homes on either bet, as the probability of winning is astronomically low in both cases.

Hence, the "three times more likely" argument — though it sounds great on a brochure or when your broker quotes it during the hard sell — is effectively irrelevant. Instead, let's look at the likelihood of suffering a disability from another perspective, one that may convince even the cynics. If we told you that you have a 10% likelihood of suffering a disability by the age of 65 — one that lasts 90 days or more — would you make the effort to protect yourself? What if the probability of the disability were 25%?

In fact, a 25-year-old has a 58% probability of suffering a disability lasting 90 days or more by the age of 65.[18] And people aged 35 and 45 have a 50% and 40% probability, respectively, of the same thing happening. The probability of

17 Commissioner's Disability Table, Society of Actuaries (1985).
18 Ibid.

suffering a disability is clearly not astronomically low — it is, unfortunately, quite probable.

How long do disabilities last? Some evidence suggests that disabilities exceeding 90 days average 2.95 years.[19] However, it is important to keep in mind that the length of the disability depends on the severity of the disability. Historical evidence suggests the following breakdown.[20] Consider 1,000 Canadians in a given year who have a disability. Of these thousand people, 443 will recover from the disability in the following year. Of those 443 lucky individuals, 336 will recover from a mild disability, 89 from a moderate disability, and only 19 from a severe disability. Of the same thousand Canadians, the remaining 557 will continue to be disabled in the following year. Of those, 355 will experience disability with the same severity as in the previous year, 102 will experience a more severe disability, and 100 will experience a less severe disability. The length of disability clearly varies greatly, depending on its severity.

Misperception 2: "The government will take care of it."

We hope you're convinced that the probability of loss caused by a disability is significant. However, some might argue that while the *probability* of loss is significant, the *magnitude* of loss is not. After all, Canadians are already protected through government programs such as Employment Insurance, Canadian Pension Plan or Quebec Pension Plan disability benefits, and workers' compensation board benefits. With all of these programs in place, do we really need to be concerned about protecting ourselves against future disabilities?

While the variety of government programs sound comforting, careful analysis suggests that potential benefits from

19 Ibid.

20 Based on the years 1989–1990. In Gail Fawcett, *Living with Disability in Canada: An Economic Portrait* (Ottawa: Human Resources and Development Canada, 1996), Figure 4.2.

government sources are limited in four ways: the individuals and disabilities covered, and the duration and amount of coverage.

Let's review those government programs. Employment Insurance benefits are offered through Human Resources Development Canada (HRDC). While we typically think of EI benefits as flowing to those who have lost their jobs, they are also paid upon sickness, injury, or quarantine. Benefits are paid for up to 15 weeks following two weeks of disability, and require a medical certificate specifying how long the illness is expected to last. The benefits are 55% of average insurable earnings, and the weekly maximum in August 2001 was $413 per week.

While useful, EI benefits alone provide insufficient protection. First, while $413 per week should not be disregarded, such an amount is not likely to support a family with a mortgage, car payments, and other bills due. Second, the duration of the protection is limited — disabilities usually last much longer than the designated time period. Third, not everyone is eligible for EI — for example, self-employed individuals.

Canadian Pension Plan (CPP) disability benefits are offered through HRDC as well, with its counterpart in the Quebec Pension Plan (QPP). CPP benefits are based on HRDC's unique definition of what constitutes a disability. First, the disability must be *severe* — that is, it must prevent you from working regularly at *any* job. Second, the disability must be *prolonged*, suggesting a long-term condition. The disability payments begin four months after the CPP finds you disabled — backdated no more than 12 months before you apply — and continue until the age of 65. According to HRDC, the average CPP disability benefit in 2000 was $684.14 per month, and the maximum benefit in August 2001 was $935.12 per month. In August 2001, a dependent child received $178.42 per month as well.

The QPP disability benefits are similar. An individual is

deemed disabled if he or she is unable to regularly pursue "substantially gainful occupation," and if the disability is likely to be "permanent." One exception is for individuals between 60 and 65, who are deemed disabled if they can no longer regularly pursue the gainful occupation they left because of the disability. The maximum QPP disability benefits were $935.09 per month in August 2001 — almost identical to the CPP. But a dependent child received $56.65 per month — much lower than the benefit offered by the CPP.

Like EI benefits, CPP/QPP disability benefits are useful. They kick in after four months — approximately when the EI benefits end. However, CPP/QPP benefits are also often insufficient. First, the amounts provided are way too low to provide adequate support. Second, the "severe and prolonged" or "permanent" definition of disability makes it difficult for many disabilities to qualify. Third, one must first be eligible for CPP/QPP to qualify. Even if you are designated as disabled, to be eligible for CPP disability benefits you must have contributed to the CPP in four of the last six years and must have earned over that period 10% of each year's maximum pensionable earnings, a value that changes each year, but was $38,300 in 2001. There are conditions under which a person may be eligible even if he or she has not made the required contributions, and self-employed individuals can choose to participate in the CPP/QPP voluntarily. However, it is fair to say that many disabled Canadians are ineligible for these benefits.

Finally, workers' compensation benefits are provincially and territorially regulated programs to compensate workers injured on the job (the names of the boards vary). The amount of benefits depends on the jurisdiction. However, many industries and jobs do not qualify for benefits, and the disability must be related to your job. For example, you do not receive benefits if you happen to fall off your bicycle on the way to work.

Besides the programs discussed above, your provincial or territorial government has a program to compensate victims of crime. This is administered through the jurisdiction's workers' compensation board or through a separate compensation board for criminal injuries.

Not surprisingly, historical evidence shows that government programs provide insufficient protection. According to the Canadian Life and Health Insurance Association (CLHIA), disabilities lead to almost half of all mortgage foreclosures. Further, historical evidence suggests that poverty rates are higher for those with disabilities.[21] A 1991 study found that poverty rates for people without disabilities were 11% and 9.5% for Canadians aged 25 to 44 and 45 to 64, respectively. During the same year, the poverty rates for those with disabilities were 22.6% and 21.8% for each age group. Further, the more severe the disability is, the higher the associated poverty rate.

As we have seen above, a number of different government programs do indeed provide benefits for the disabled. However, once you consider eligibility, the amount provided, and the duration of the payments, you would be well-advised to consider alternative sources of protection as well.

Besides the government programs discussed above, you may also have some disability coverage from a group plan — possibly at work — as do close to eight million Canadians. However, if you are like most people, you are likely unaware of the details of your plan. Does it apply to long-term or short-term disabilities? When does it kick in? Are there any restrictions or exclusions you should be aware of? It may be that your group plan is more than adequate and no further coverage is required. On the other hand, why wait until a disability happens before you find out? It's important to be fully informed

21 Ibid., Figures 5.2 and 5.3.

— before it's too late.

Disability insurance through a group plan typically lasts only as long as you keep your job. What will you do if you quit your job, go on strike, or are terminated? If you are planning to quit your job and go it alone, you may wish to consider the implications such a decision will have for your disability coverage, *before* you make a drastic decision.

We hope that we've convinced you that protection against disability should be seriously considered. The likelihood of disability is high and the likely duration of disability is lengthy. Furthermore, existing government programs may provide limited or no protection, so the potential magnitude of loss is considerable. If the objective of insurance is to protect your family's standard of living after an unexpected event, then protecting your family against loss of income because of a disability falls in line with that objective.

How Does Disability Insurance Work?

The purpose of disability insurance is to provide you with a regular monthly income to replace income received from work should you be unable to work because of a disability. In theory, therefore, disability insurance should be quite straightforward. In practice, however, policies that sound superficially similar may differ greatly with regard to how disability is defined, when benefits are received, how large are the benefits, and whether the insurance company can cancel or change the policy. Let's deal with each of these issues in turn.

When and How Long Are Benefits Received?

A disability policy will specify an elimination period. This refers to the period of time between the occurrence of the disability and the beginning of payments. The elimination period is an important factor in determining the total cost of the policy. In many ways, it is similar to the deductible associated with property insurance. As we discussed in earlier chapters, a high deductible reduces costs to the insurance company by eliminating numerous small, yet administratively costly, claims. The same applies to the elimination period.

The choice of elimination period may be related to other disability coverage the policyholder holds. For example, if you have sufficient short-term coverage through government programs, you may decide to specify an elimination period that will cause the insurance benefits to kick in when the other benefits stop.

The policy will also specify the length of coverage. A short-term policy may last two years, while a long-term policy may last until the age of 65. When specifying the length of coverage, keep in mind that if a disability has lasted, say, eight years, recovery is unlikely to take place in the immediate future. Hence, it makes little sense to specify medium-term coverage. If you wish to protect yourself against eight years of disability, you will likely require coverage until age 65.

How Is "Disability" Defined?

More than any other consideration, the way your policy defines the term "disability" will determine the nature of the policy — and whether you actually receive benefits. After suffering a disability, many policyholders are disappointed to find that it is not covered. But they could have protected themselves easily by simply reading the fine print before signing. The insurance companies are not completely blameless either; without question, policies can be confusing.

Here are some details. The policy may define disabilities in terms of occupation. Hence, disability may be determined by whether it renders a person unable to perform his or her "own occupation," "regular occupation," or "any occupation." "Own occupation" refers to the job the individual had before the disability. "Regular occupation" refers to any job within the individual's profession. "Any occupation" refers to any occupation *for which the individual is qualified* by education and experience.

Alternatively, the policy may define disability in terms of forgone earnings. In this context, it may be defined as "total disability" or "residual disability." For total disability, the policy provides benefits only if you are unable to work *at all*, the most restrictive definition. Residual disability applies to a situation in which the policyholder is able to work, but suffers a decrease in income because of the disability. The insured is typically required to have sustained a decrease in income of at least 20% for the benefits to kick in.

The insurance policy may include other provisions and riders. For example, it may provide benefits for "presumptive total disability." This refers to the total or permanent loss from disease or injury of the use of a faculty or of more than one limb. Loss of speech, hearing, eyesight, both hands, both feet, or two limbs would render an insured presumptively totally disabled. As another example, a "partial disability" rider might specify that the policyholder receive 50% of the monthly benefit if he or she sustains continuous loss of at least 50% of the time required for regular daily duties.

Depending on the wording of the policy, a disability caused by a pre-existing condition may or may not be covered, even if the condition was not known to exist at the time the contract was signed. Consider the following example. An individual takes out a disability insurance contract. One year later, the policyholder falls ill and makes a disability claim. An independent diagnosis by the insurance company's doctor determines that the illness is due to a condition that has been developing for several years. Under some policies, the policyholder would receive disability benefits, since the *symptoms* of the pre-existing condition appeared only after the contract was in effect. Under other policies, however, he or she would not receive benefits, since the condition existed when the contract was signed, albeit unknown to the policyholder.

But what happens if a pre-existing condition is known about at the time the contract is signed? In that case, the condition would be excluded. For example, a person with chronic lower back pain will be able to obtain only insurance that explicitly excludes disabilities associated with the lower back. However, should the individual develop a disability of another part of the back, benefits would be paid, because there would be no relationship between the disability and the pre-existing condition.

As well, the policy could apply to disabilities caused by both illness and accident, or caused by illnesses exclusively. And just in case things aren't confusing enough, the policy may use more than one definition of disability at the same time or for different time periods. For example, while "own occupation" and "residual disability" may apply for the first two years of disability, "any occupation" may apply thereafter. While the differences between some of these definitions may seem trivial, we guarantee this: Your insurance company will pay close attention to them, and will refuse to pay benefits if your disability doesn't precisely match the definition in the insurance contract.

Insurance companies are also rigorous about confirming that you do indeed have a disability. This is fair — many illnesses and injuries are difficult to diagnose objectively, and no two people are affected by the same illness in the same way. A soft-tissue injury — a sprain or strain, such as a shoulder injury — may result in a two-week disability for one person, but could disable another individual for half a year. At a bare minimum, the insurance company will want a statement regarding your disability from your doctor, and may want an independent doctor to examine you as well.

How Large Are the Benefits?

The insurance company specifies a maximum amount of insurance that a policyholder is allowed to acquire. The company will typically base maximum benefits on pre-disability income, occupation type, and age. Disability insurance benefits are typically less than 70% of pre-disability income. Superficially, the specifying of maximum benefits seems counterintuitive — isn't the purpose of disability insurance to protect policyholders against the loss of income-earning power? And doesn't the insurance company want as much of your business as possible? The rationale behind maximum benefits is that it creates an "incentive gap" between the amount you earn by working and the amount you receive from disability benefits. The insurance companies hope that the gap will motivate people back into the workforce and prevent faking or exaggeration of disability (that is, moral hazard).

Note, however, that personally owned and personally paid individual disability insurance benefits are generally tax-free — unlike the premiums. Hence, the after-tax difference between pre-disability income and disability benefits is not necessarily large. On the other hand, people with disabilities typically face higher expenses. They may have to use taxis more often, may require home care, or may wish to participate in an experimental medical procedure in another country.

Inflation is another important consideration. It may be possible to purchase a cost-of-living rider, which indexes benefits to inflation. A similar-sounding, yet different rider is a pre-disability indexing benefit, which automatically indexes benefits — and premiums — to changes in the policyholder's earnings.

The benefits received from individual disability insurance are typically integrated with government and group disability benefits. Hence, the disability insurance benefits kick in only when required to provide protection not covered by workers' compensation, for example.

Can the Insurance Company Cancel or Change the Policy?

There are three types of disability insurance contracts: cancellable contracts, guaranteed renewable contracts, and contracts that are both non-cancellable and guaranteed renewable. A cancellable contract allows the insurance provider to reserve the right to change the premiums and coverage, refuse renewal, or add exclusions or restrictions.

Table 4.2
Types of Disability Insurance Contracts

Type of Contract	Premiums	Coverage	Renewal
Cancellable	Insurer can modify	Insurer can modify	Insurer can refuse to renew, or renew with restrictions or exclusions
Guaranteed renewable	Insurer can modify for an entire class	Insurer cannot modify	Guaranteed
Non-cancellable and guaranteed	Insurer cannot modify	Insurer cannot modify	Guaranteed

A guaranteed renewable contract offers more protection than a cancellable contract. The insurer agrees not to modify the coverage or refuse renewability. However, the insurance company can modify the premium, but only for an entire class of policyholders. The insurer cannot arbitrarily decide to increase a single individual's premiums, but can choose, for example, to increase premiums for all female smokers in northwest Ontario.

A non-cancellable and guaranteed renewable contract offers the most complete protection. The premium and coverage, which are determined at contract issuance, cannot be changed until a specified age. There are exceptions, however; in the case of fraud or misrepresentation during a period of contestability, such as the first 24 months after signing, the contract is cancellable.

How Does Critical Illness Insurance Work?

Unfortunately, we all face a significant probability of suffering a critical illness in our lifetime. According to the Heart and Stroke Foundation of Canada, there are over 75,000 heart attacks and 50,000 strokes in Canada each year. And according to the Canadian Cancer Society, an estimated 134,100 new cases of cancer will occur in Canada in 2001. But, thanks to the miracles of modern medicine, a heart attack, stroke, or cancer is not an immediate death penalty. In fact, over 80% of heart attack victims admitted to hospital survive; the death rate for hospitalized heart attack victims has decreased from 16% to 8% in recent years. There are close to 300,000 stroke survivors in Canada, and 60% of them have been left with disabilities. Survival rates for cancer have increased as well. Indeed, should you be diagnosed with cancer or suffer a heart attack or stroke, the probability of survival is high. This is obviously good news, but as survival rates increase, the need for critical illness insurance increases as well.

Critical illness insurance was first introduced in South Africa in 1983, and in Canada in the 1990s. It provides a single, tax-free, lump-sum payment to be used as desired by the insured person once he or she has been diagnosed with a critical illness. The mechanics of critical illness insurance is similar to life insurance, except that it's a critical illness, not death, that triggers the benefit. A very good, if trivial, argument can be made that critical illness insurance provides real life insurance, while life insurance actually provides only death insurance! As with life insurance, the policy may provide term or permanent coverage. Critical illness can also be attached to a life insurance plan. Interestingly, more critical illness policies are sold in South Africa and the United Kingdom than life insurance policies.[22]

Most critical illness policies cover heart attack, life-threatening cancer, and stroke. Examples of additional illnesses that may be covered are Alzheimer's disease, blindness, coma, coronary artery bypass, deafness, kidney failure, loss of limbs, loss of speech, major organ transplant, motor neuron disease, multiple sclerosis, occupational HIV infection, paralysis, Parkinson's disease, and severe burns. Of course, you must read the fine print; different insurance companies may define illnesses differently. A more expensive policy may be so because of a more liberal definition of illness, and vice versa.

Critical illness insurance policies typically specify a period following diagnosis that the policyholder must survive before a claim can be made. This eliminates situations in which the policyholder could conceivably receive both critical illness and life insurance payments for the same health condition. For example, without such a waiting period, if a person holding both critical illness and life insurance coverage had a heart attack and died the next day, the insurance company would be required to satisfy both policies. This may sound like an extra bonus for the

22 *Edmonton Journal* (December 28, 2000).

beneficiaries — but the policyholder would pay for it through higher premiums.

As discussed earlier, we all face a significant probability of developing a critical illness in our lifetime. Some people may nevertheless feel that critical illness insurance is a waste of money (a feeling that evaporates quickly once such an illness is diagnosed). In response to this concern, the policy may include an option to return the premiums paid if a claim has not been made by a certain age or before death. In the case of death, the premiums are refunded to the beneficiary of the deceased. An extra premium is, of course, charged for this option.

Which One Is for Me?

There is no simple answer when deciding whether to purchase disability or critical illness insurance — or when deciding how much of each to purchase. Let's assume that you've shopped around in the competitive insurance market. Based on your survey, you've found the best possible price for the types of disability and critical illness insurance policies you are considering buying. Given the existence of a competitive market, it's unlikely that there is a pure financial advantage to either type of policy. In other words, we would probably not be able to compare the risk and time-adjusted value of the cash flows associated with each type of policy and magically conclude that one is "cheaper."

If we could predict the future, we would choose critical illness insurance for a short-term disability caused by illness, as the lump-sum payment from the insurance company is obligatory even if the policyholder recovers. Similarly, we would prefer disability insurance for a longer-term disability or for one that is not caused by a critical illness, as the monthly payments would continue throughout the period of disability. However, we can't predict the future. The decision about which to buy has to be based on personal preference and lifestyle. There are convincing arguments in support of each type of insurance.

One argument in support of disability insurance is that it is more comprehensive than critical illness insurance, as it provides benefits for a wider range of disabilities. A strained back or depression may not qualify as a critical illness, but either could make you unable to work for a long period of time.

Another argument in support of disability insurance is that, while critical illness insurance policies pay a lump-sum benefit upon diagnosis, once the benefit has been issued, the contract is terminated. Therefore the policyholder can claim for only one critical illness; any subsequent illnesses will not be covered. Disability insurance, on the other hand, pays the policyholder monthly benefits for as long as the disability persists (within the time constraints specified in the contract). If the policyholder continues to satisfy the terms of the contract, the policy remains in force and subsequent claims may be submitted.

But many people don't qualify for disability insurance. Stay-at-home parents, homemakers, and caregivers don't qualify, as they don't receive an "official" income. This may surprise some people because, although no official income is received, stay-at-home parents, homemakers, and caregivers do, in fact, work, and they contribute significantly to family income through reduction of costs and increased quality of life. Insurance companies are reluctant to provide disability insurance for those working at home because it is difficult, if a claim is made, for them to ascertain whether the claimant is truly disabled and unable to work. Even people who work from home with an official income sometimes have difficulty obtaining disability insurance, for this very reason. There are also occupations not based at home that are typically not considered insurable for individual disability insurance. These include actors, singers, authors, performers in carnivals or circuses, models, carwash and parking lot employees, manicurists, professional athletes, and many others.

An argument in support of critical illness insurance is that while the benefits received for both types of insurance can be used at the beneficiary's discretion, the lump-sum payment from critical illness insurance allows the beneficiary much greater flexibility. For example, many people who are critically ill seek to travel outside of Canada for medical procedures. One reason for leaving the country is that certain experimental procedures may be unavailable in Canada. Another reason often cited is the extensive waiting lists for some medical procedures in Canada. On the other hand, critical illness insurance may be used to pay off a mortgage.

Consider a person with cancer who wishes to travel to Mexico for an experimental procedure costing $100,000 Canadian. Without critical illness insurance, this individual would have two choices. One would be to withdraw the funds from the family's savings. However, double the required amount might have to be withdrawn if it came from an RRSP. After all, cash withdrawn from an RRSP is taxable (unless it is part of the Home Buyer plan) and therefore more cash has to be withdrawn from the RRSP than actually required. For example, in the case of a 50% tax rate, $200,000 must be withdrawn if $100,000 is required. The cancer patient's second choice is to forgo the procedure. While we may personally question the effectiveness of some experimental procedures, many policyholders wish to have the freedom to make their own choices, and a lump sum provides this flexibility.

Another reason to consider critical illness insurance instead of disability insurance is that, even if you are diagnosed with a critical illness, you may not immediately be unable to work. But you may wish to spend time with your family instead of working to support them during this traumatic time. This is particularly true of life-threatening illnesses such as cancer.

Another argument in support of critical illness insurance over disability insurance is that critical illness insurance benefits are triggered by a clearly defined insurable event — an objectively diagnosed critical illness. Disability insurance, on the other hand, is triggered by a less clean-cut insurable event. For example, as discussed earlier, soft-tissue injuries are difficult to diagnose objectively. That a clearly defined insurable event triggers critical illness insurance benefits is useful for two distinct reasons. First, adverse selection is less of an issue with critical illness, as it is difficult to predict or exaggerate the insurable event. Second, because the event is clearly defined, there is less chance of being rejected, in contrast with disability insurance, which may depend on a subjective diagnosis.

As you can see, there are strong arguments in favour of both disability and critical illness insurance. The ultimate decision depends on which considerations are most important to you and your lifestyle. For example, people in occupations that depend less on physical capabilities, such as lawyers and academics, may be less concerned about disability and more concerned about having cash available should they suffer a critical illness. A cabinetmaker or hairdresser, on the other hand, may be more concerned about a disability, which could effectively end a skilled worker's career in his or her chosen profession. High-income earners who wish to exceed the maximum disability benefit level for their occupations may want to use critical illness insurance as well.

At a more general level, your choice is not only between critical illness insurance and disability insurance. These two forms of insurance can work together with life insurance (Chapter 1) and private health insurance (Chapter 3), to form part of your family's strategy to provide protection should tragedy strike. The four types of insurance are each intended to satisfy one of two general objectives: replacing income or paying for expenses related to disability. Disability insurance and life insurance are primarily perceived as income replacement, though critical illness insurance may play this role as well. Private health coverage and critical illness insurance are primarily perceived as paying for expenses associated with disability, although life insurance may be used to pay for expenses associated with death.

Can you live without one or two of these types of insurance? For most of us, the answer is yes. For example, life insurance may include *accelerated living benefits*, which allow terminally ill policyholders to access their insurance benefits while alive. As well, some Canadian jurisdictions permit *viatical settlements*, in which a terminally ill person (the viator) can sell his or her rights under a life insurance policy to a third party (the viatical settlement provider) in exchange for cash payments. (The term "viatical" is derived from *viaticum*, a Latin word that means "provisions for a long journey.") As another example, you may wish to forgo private health care coverage and instead use critical illness insurance to cover medical expenses. However, in all the examples above, there are still gaps in coverage. You may be critically ill, but not terminally ill, and will not receive accelerated living benefits. Or you may have an illness not specified in the critical illness insurance contract, and therefore not have cash to cover your medical expenses.

Of course, if we could afford to do so, we would purchase all four types of insurance in order to ensure coverage in every possible situation. Unfortunately, most of us do not have enough free cash flow to buy everything we wish, which constrains our choices. However, careful planning can permit more flexibility than you may realize is possible when making insurance choices.

As a specific example, let's consider disability insurance, which tends to require the policyholder to make a number of choices regarding coverage. The policyholder pays (in additional premiums) every time a choice is made that provides additional options, because those options place further obligations on the insurer. Choosing a policy that defines a disability according to "any occupation" rather than "own occupation" will be cheaper, because the liberal "own occupation" definition provides the policyholder with much greater flexibility when disabled, thereby placing a further burden on the insurer. Similarly, choosing a disability policy with a longer elimination period will drastically reduce the premiums, as discussed earlier. If given the choice between waiting an extra three months for the disability insurance to kick in, or $50,000 of extra critical illness insurance, which would you choose?

The decisions associated with protecting yourself against future disability are very personal, and often difficult to make. However, given the constraints on your ability to pay premiums, truly understanding your choices — understanding what you *really* need and what are simply bells and whistles — will put you in a better position to make insurance decisions that maximize future benefits.

Summary Points

- The need to acquire disability insurance and/or critical illness insurance is often overlooked. This is because of two common misperceptions: "I'll never be disabled" and "The government will take care of it." The probability and likely duration of future disability are high, although the duration of the disability is a function of its severity. There are government programs that can help, such as Employment

Insurance (EI), Canada Pension Plan (CPP) or Quebec Pension Plan (QPP) disability benefits, and workers' compensation benefits. Nonetheless, government programs are limited in terms of who and what disabilities are covered, as well as the duration and amount of coverage.

- The purpose of disability insurance is to provide regular monthly income to replace income received from work in case an individual is unable to work because of a disability. How-ever, policies vary widely with regard to when benefits are received, how disability is defined, the size of benefits, and whether the insurance company can cancel or change the policy.
- Critical illness insurance, a relative newcomer to Canada, provides a single, tax-free, lump-sum payment once the insured has been diagnosed with a critical illness such as heart attack, stroke, or cancer, among others. The need for critical illness insurance is highlighted by the significant and increasing probability of suffering and surviving a critical illness.
- Arguments can be made for and against both disability insurance and critical illness insurance. Disability insurance is more comprehensive and remains in force following a disability. But many people are ineligible for disability insurance and may choose critical illness insurance instead. Further, the critical illness lump-sum payment provides the policyholder with flexibility that is unavailable with monthly disability insurance payments, in terms of both discretionary availability of cash and being able to receive the benefit even if the policyholder can work.
- Given cash-flow constraints, disability insurance, critical illness insurance, private health insurance, and life insurance in various combinations satisfy the dual objectives of income replacement and expense coverage.

How to Sound Intelligent

Some Questions to Ask When Purchasing Disability Insurance

- How long is the elimination period?
- For how long are the benefits received?
- How does the policy define disability?
- What are the maximum benefits allowed?
- How are the benefits integrated with government or group benefits I may receive?
- What is the tax status of the premiums and benefits?
- How does the policy treat unknown and known pre-existing conditions?
- Can the insurance company cancel or change the policy?
- What riders and provisions are available?

Some Questions to Ask When Purchasing Critical Illness Insurance

- What critical illnesses are covered, and how are they defined?
- What is the lump-sum payment if I become critically ill?
- How long must I survive the critical illness in order to collect?
- Is my coverage term or permanent?
- What riders and provisions are available?

5

Automobile Insurance

You've paid your latest automobile insurance bill, but you just don't understand it. After all, you, your spouse, and your 18-year-old son have never had an accident — and you paid both of those speeding tickets promptly. Yet the cash you are forking over to the insurance company for your two cars seems more appropriate for a Grand Prix racing car driver with a frequent crash record than for a suburban family!

Why does automobile insurance cost so much? Why are there such dramatic variations in price between rival companies? And why is it mandatory? These questions have probably crossed the mind of every automobile owner at one time or another. Our goal in this chapter is to try to answer these questions and to explain why the prudent consumer is well-advised to do a little comparison shopping before committing to a specific insurer or a specific policy. Many consumers purchase automobile insurance with little or no understanding of how their lifestyle choices affect insurance prices. Insurance premiums vary considerably, depending on your driving habits, the type of automobile you own, and many other factors. Further, policyholders are likely to receive highly disparate price quotes from different insurance companies. For this reason, it's important to develop a clear understanding of the various factors that underlie prices.

In Canada, it is mandatory to have some automobile insurance. However, the minimum compulsory insurance coverage varies greatly from jurisdiction to jurisdiction — and don't think for a second that you aren't financially vulnerable if you hold only the minimum amount of coverage. Before we explore similarities and differences across jurisdictions — and why automobile insurance is mandatory in the first place — let's explore the different parties in the automobile insurance game and the concepts of legal liability and "no-fault" insurance.

Parties and Legal Liability

Automobile insurance policies provide protection against legal liability associated with an automobile accident, as well as compensation for bodily injuries. Canadian law distinguishes between three "parties" with regard to legal liability and automobile insurance: the first party, the second party, and the third party. The *first party*, also referred to as the *named insured*, is simply you, the policyholder — the individual in whose name the policy is issued. The *second party* refers to the insurance company that issues the policy. The *third party* is someone you should hope never to be involved with, since it refers to another person with whom you are involved in an accident.

If you are involved in an accident, you may face *legal liability* — a requirement to compensate the third party for your negligent driving. For example, if you drove through a red light and hit another automobile in the intersection, causing a fatality, there's a pretty good chance that you would be found negligent.

To determine whether you were in fact negligent, your behaviour would be compared to that of a "reasonable and prudent" individual in similar circumstances. Of course, the definition of "reasonable and prudent" permits some flexibility, but ample case law can be called upon to make such a judgement.

Some people might argue that liability insurance is not good for society. After all, society makes us legally liable for our actions behind the wheel for two reasons: to motivate us to avoid actions that may result in liability, and to compensate the victims of our actions. Liability insurance lessens the motivation to avoid actions that may result in liability. Hence, it effectively undercuts one of the major reasons for its existence.

There are, however, a number of reasons why protection against automobile-related liability is good for society. First, while the financial implications of an accident are lessened by liability insurance, the insured person will continue to be careful when driving because of the bodily injury he or she might suffer should an accident occur. Second, an individual involved in an accident does face some financial burden — in terms of higher future premiums — albeit much less than the financial implications of getting into an accident without insurance. Third, because premiums are a function of the driver's potential for legal liability — that is, his or her potential for getting into an accident — certain high-risk drivers are unable to drive because they are unable to afford the high premiums for mandatory automobile insurance.

The fourth, and most important, reason why liability insurance is good for society is that in many situations, the compensation that an individual has to pay because of legal liability could be enormous — well beyond the financial means of the average person. And, unfortunately, damage to people or property caused by negligent driving is all too common. Without an insurance system, the human tragedies associated with automobile accidents would become even greater — the injured third party would not receive compensation and the negligent first party would face financial ruin, to say nothing of the physical injuries they may have suffered.

No-Fault Insurance

As early as the 1930s, experts were voicing criticisms of the traditional insurance system, in which insurers accepted responsibility for policyholder liability. The purpose of the liability system, you'll recall, is to fairly compensate third parties who are victims of the first parties' negligence. But numerous inefficiencies are involved in this process.

First, determining negligence typically involves an expensive legal process that requires lawyers for each party. The cost of lawyers is high, thereby limiting the actual compensation received by victims and raising the cost of doing business for the insurers. Much of the cost associated with these legal battles is passed on to customers. In a truly efficient system, delivering compensation would not involve these high costs.

Second, the number and complexity of legal cases inevitably result in long delays, which clearly do little to help innocent third parties. In a more efficient system, claims are settled expeditiously, so that compensation is delivered to the third parties as soon as possible.

Third, legal confrontations tie up governmental and court resources that might otherwise be used for better purposes. Inefficiencies in the liability insurance system also create delays for other legal cases, and the resulting costs are passed on to taxpayers.

Fourth, the use of courts and juries occasionally yields verdicts that many experts regard as unfair. Some third parties receive huge settlements, well beyond their deserved compensation. Others in similar circumstances receive very little. Why the difference? Well, the comparative abilities of their lawyers is one obvious factor. And the random selection of jurors — some more sympathetic, some less — is another. While the justice system in most Western nations is highly respected, wide discrepancies in compensation raise serious questions about its efficiency in determining negligence.

These inefficiencies result in a substandard system — that is, substandard to a system in which proving negligence and determining proper compensation are done at the lowest possible cost and as quickly as possible. To address these issues, no-fault automobile insurance laws have been implemented in some quarters and advocated in many others. Of course, the term "no-fault" is somewhat misleading, because the at-fault party will likely have to deal with increased premiums. But it is no-fault in this sense: Compensation is paid out independently of determination of fault. It can be paid even when no fault is found. In exchange, in most situations there is an effective cap on how much the insurance companies have to pay out.

Here's how it works. Under no-fault insurance laws, policyholders receive certain monetary benefits depending on the severity of the accident. In return, they generally forfeit the right to sue. The benefits of this system are obvious. Lawyers and the court system are largely uninvolved, so there is little risk of either unfairly high or unfairly low cash disbursements. A disadvantage to the insurance company is that it could end up paying out for claims for which it was not really responsible. For example, the policyholder may not, in fact, have been negligent in the accident. Had the case proceeded through the courts, the insurance company might have received a judgement in its favour. Under the no-fault insurance system, the company must still pay compensation. A disadvantage to the injured party is that the final compensation could be considerably less than what he or she might have received in court from a sympathetic jury.

The efficiency benefits of a no-fault insurance system are obvious. But a fascinating study suggests that its benefits may also be medical in nature. In April 2000, a group of Canadian medical researchers published an article in the prestigious *New England Journal of Medicine* that reported a 28% reduction in the number of whiplash injury claims following Saskatchewan's 1995 change from a tort-compensation system to a no-fault system.[23] Further, the time period in which claims were settled decreased from 433 days to 194 days. Most interestingly, they found that the amount of pain and suffering that injury victims reported was closely associated with how much time passed until claims were settled — both before and after the change to a no-fault system.

We can think of a number of possible explanations for these results. A cynic might argue that in a no-fault system, individuals who might otherwise fraudulently exaggerate a whiplash injury — to take advantage of the pain-and-suffering legal-lottery boondoggle — simply no longer bother. A less cynical explanation is that the tort-compensation system shuffles the injured party from doctor to doctor, from lawyer to lawyer, and possibly from courtroom to courtroom. When you are forced to spend over a year defending the existence of an injury, it's difficult to get it out of your mind, an important component of recovery. Whichever explanation is the true one — they both may hold a grain of truth — one conclusion is clear. The implementation of a no-fault system may have benefits — and, potentially, costs such as moral hazard — that are beyond pure efficiency.

In practice, no-fault automobile insurance laws vary greatly

23 Please see "Sources and Further Reading" for the detailed reference.

from province to province. As we will discuss below, in Manitoba and Quebec all lawsuits are forbidden; elsewhere, lawsuits are permitted. But even in provinces where litigation is possible, several conditions restrain full use of the court system.

Mandatory Automobile Insurance

With the exception of automobile insurance, the decision to purchase insurance is, from a legal perspective, optional. Consider life insurance. While it may be very *advisable* for someone supporting a live-at-home spouse and five children under the age of 10 to purchase life insurance, no law forces such an individual to do so. However, should the same person drive an automobile without the mandatory automobile insurance, she or he might face heavy fines and license suspension. What's going on here?

The answer is threefold.

First, an individual with many dependants has obvious motivation to purchase life insurance. Without it, upon that person's death, the spouse might have to sell the family home and/or find a job, and the children might have to borrow money to attend university. Conversely, there is less motivation to purchase automobile insurance, because it is meant to protect individuals (almost always strangers) with whom the person may someday be involved in an accident.

Second, the household financial burden associated with an individual's death could be difficult in terms of loss of the income that he or she generated while alive. However, the potential damage in terms of liability that the same person can cause with an automobile is much larger, and much more burdensome to society. The legal costs alone associated with determining fault would likely bankrupt many households. Hence, the potential magnitude of loss is large. Without mandatory insurance, the victims of automobile accidents would be very unlikely to see much compensation from the individuals at fault.

Third, the government can suspend an individual's right to a driving license, which gives it a degree of leverage when enforcing mandatory insurance laws. No similar leverage applies to life insurance. Another scenario in which one party can force another to purchase insurance involves mortgages, for which home insurance is usually a required condition. This is another example in which an external party — the mortgage provider — uses its leverage (pun intended) to force you to make insurance decisions that are in its own best interest.

Exactly which types of automobile insurance are mandatory varies greatly across provincial and territorial jurisdictions. Also, as governments are voted in and out of office and as politicians change legislation, variations in mandatory automobile insurance occur over time. In most jurisdictions, however, the minimum compulsory insurance coverage includes the following:

- *Third party liability coverage* — allows you to compensate a third party for your negligent driving.
- *Statutory accident benefits* — provide limited compensation to you, the driver, for the financial burdens associated with an accident, and include medical payments and disability, funeral, and death benefits.
- *Uninsured automobile coverage* — provides limited compensation if you are injured or killed by an uninsured driver or unidentified vehicle. This coverage, providing up to $200,000, is universal in Canada. In Quebec, coverage is granted by the Fonds d'indemnisation administered by the Société de l'assurance automobile du Québec.

In some jurisdictions, additional insurance is also compulsory. For example, in Ontario and Quebec, *direct compensation property damage* insurance is required, which allows the policyholder to collect directly from his or her own insurer should someone else damage the vehicle. Table 5.1 uses information from the Insurance Bureau of Canada to explore similarities and differences in minimum compulsory insurance coverage. Note that this information is current as of July 2001; we advise you to check with your jurisdiction to determine if any changes have taken place since then.

As we can see from Table 5.1, Canadian law requires you (the first party) to acquire third party liability insurance. In most provinces and territories, you must carry at least $200,000 of third party liability insurance. The exception is Quebec, where the minimum limit is $50,000 (in Quebec, liability insurance is referred to as civil liability insurance). Medical payments per person vary wildly — from $10,000 in Alberta and Yukon to an unlimited amount in Manitoba and Quebec. Funeral benefits range from $1,000 (in Newfoundland, Northwest Territories, Nunavut, Nova Scotia, and Prince Edward Island) to $6,000 in Ontario, which raises a question — do funerals cost six times more in Ontario than in Nova Scotia? Let's hope we don't have to answer that question anytime soon!

Similar differences exist with regard to the other variables listed in the table. Of particular interest to people involved in an accident — and their lawyers — is whether any restrictions exist on their right to sue the at-fault party for damages. With the exception of Manitoba, Quebec, and Saskatchewan, an individual involved in an accident can sue for pain and suffering. With regard to economic loss in excess of no-fault benefits, an individual involved in an accident can sue in every jurisdiction except Manitoba and Quebec.

Table 5.1

Minimum Compulsory Automobile Insurance Coverage, July 2001

Jurisdiction	Third Party Liability[1]	Medical Payments per Person[2]	Funeral Expense Benefits	Disability Income Benefits (% of wages)[3,4]	Sue for Pain and Suffering	Sue for Economic Loss over No-Fault Benefits	Administration[5]
Alberta (AB)	$200,000	$10,000	$2,000	80% of gross; max. $300/week	yes	yes	private insurers
British Columbia (BC)	$200,000	$150,000	$2,500	75% of gross; max. $300/week	yes	yes	government
Manitoba (MB)	$200,000	unlimited	$3,803	90% of net	no	no	government
New Brunswick (NB)	$200,000	$50,000	$2,500	max. $250/week	yes	yes	private insurers
Newfoundland (NF)[6]	$200,000	$25,000[6]	$1,000[6]	max. $140/week[6]	yes	yes	private insurers
Northwest Territories (NT) / Nunavut (NU)	$200,000	$25,000	$1,000	80% of gross; max. $140/week	yes	yes	private insurers
Nova Scotia (NS)	$200,000	$25,000	$1,000	max. $140/week	yes	yes	private insurers
Ontario (ON)	$200,000	$100,000	$6,000	80% of net; max. $400/week	yes[7]	yes[8]	private insurers
Prince Edward Island (PE)	$200,000	$25,000	$1,000	max. $140/week	yes	yes	private insurers
Quebec (QC)	$50,000	unlimited	$3,650	90% of net	no	no	government & private[9]
Saskatchewan (SK)	$200,000	$526,970	$5,270	90% of net	no	yes[10]	government
Yukon Territory (YT)	$200,000	$10,000	$2,000	80% of gross; max. $300/week	yes	yes	private insurers

Minimum Compulsory Automobile Insurance Coverage, July 2001 cont.

Jurisdiction	Death Benefits[11]
Alberta (AB)	Head of household: $10,000 plus $2,000 for each dependant after first and 1% of total principal sum for 104 weeks; no limit Spouse: $10,000 Dependent child: according to age; maximum $3,000
British Columbia (BC)	Head of household: $5,000 and $145/week for 104 weeks to first survivor, plus $1,000 and $35/week for 104 weeks for each survivor after first; no limit Spouse: $2,500 Dependent child: according to age; maximum $1,500
Manitoba (MB)	Depends on wage and age Minimum $43,466, maximum $292,500, plus $20,646–$38,032 to dependants according to age Head of household: $50,000 plus $1,000 each for all dependants beyond first
New Brunswick (NB)	Spouse: $25,000 Dependent child: $5,000
Newfoundland (NF)[6]	Head of household: $10,000 plus $1,000 each for all dependants beyond first Spouse: $10,000 Dependent child: $2,000
Northwest Territories (NT) / Nunavut (NU)	Head of household: $10,000 Spouse: $10,000 Each survivor after first: $2,500; if one survivor, spouse, or dependant, principal sum increased by $1,500
Nova Scotia (NS)	Head of household: $10,000 plus $1,000 each for all dependants beyond first Spouse: $10,000 Dependent child: $2,000
Ontario (ON)	Spouse: $25,000 Surviving dependant or for loss of dependant: $10,000

Minimum Compulsory Automobile Insurance Coverage, July 2001 cont.

Jurisdiction	Death Benefits[11]
Prince Edward Island (PE)	Head of household: $10,000 plus $1,000 each for all dependants beyond first Spouse: $10,000 Dependent child: $2,000
Quebec (QC)	Depends on wage and age Minimum $48,683, maximum $250,000, plus $23,123–$45,198 to dependants according to age If no dependants: $18,256 to parents
Saskatchewan (SK)	Spouse/dependants: $47,427 minimum; otherwise $10,539 Educational benefit: $31,618 Head of household: $10,000 plus $2,000 for each dependant after first and 1% of total principal sum for 104 weeks; no limit
Yukon Territory (YT)	Spouse: $10,000 Dependent child: according to age; maximum $3,000

Notes to Table 5.1

1. If a claim involving both bodily injury and property damage reaches this figure, payment for property damage is capped at $10,000 (AB, NT/NU, NS, ON, PE, SK, YT) or $20,000 (BC, MB, NB, NF). For QC, liability limits relate to property damage claims within QC and to personal injury and property damage claims outside QC.
2. Includes rehabilitation and excludes amounts from medical health insurance and hospital plans. For ON, $1 million if injury "catastrophic"; attendant care, $72,000 ($1 million if injury "catastrophic"). Time limit is 2 years (AB, YT), 4 years (NB, NF, NT/NU, NS, PE), or none (MB, QC). Information not provided for other jurisdictions.
3. AB, BC, YT: 104 weeks temporary or total disability. MB: maximum income $58,500/year gross; impairment benefits scheduled up to $108,664. NB, NF, NS, PE, NT/NU: 104 weeks temporary disability; lifetime if totally disabled. ON: $185/week for those not employed (104 weeks maximum or longer if victim is unable to pursue any suitable occupation). QC: maximum income $50,000/year gross: temporary, 3 years; permanent lifetime,

indexed; impairment benefits scheduled up to $137,210. SK: maximum income $54,893/year gross, indexed.

4. Unpaid housekeeper or homemaker: $70/week (NF, NS, PE), $100/week (AB, NB, NT/NU, YT), or $145/week (BC) for a maximum of 12 weeks (NF, NT/NU, NS, PE), 26 weeks (AB, YT), 52 weeks (NB), or 104 weeks (BC).
5. In BC, MB, and SK, government and private insurers compete for optional and excess coverage.
6. NF does not require you to purchase accident benefits coverage. The information provided is for the standard policy.
7. If injury meets verbal threshold, deductible applies. Lawsuit allowed only if injured person dies or sustains "permanent serious" disfigurement and/or impairment of important physical, mental, or psychological function. The court is directed to assess damages, then deduct $15,000 ($7,500 if Family Law Act claim).
8. Injured person may sue for 80% of net income loss before trial or 100% of gross after trial, also for medical, rehabilitation, and related costs when injury is "catastrophic."
9. Bodily injury: government; property damage: private insurers.
10. With respect to loss of income, they may recover only with respect to gross income losses that exceed $52,058/year; award is net of income taxes.
11. Death: anytime (AB, BC, MB, QC, YT), within 2 years (NB, NF, NS, PE, NT/NU), or within 3 years (ON). Information not provided for SK.

Source: Insurance Bureau of Canada

As its name suggests, the liability insurance agreement obligates the second party (the insurance company) to make the required payment if the first party is found legally liable for an accident. But if the compensation required is larger than the amount of insurance carried by the policyholder, the first party is personally responsible for the difference. Hence, for most people, simply purchasing the mandatory automobile insurance is insufficient.

Here's an example. You, the policyholder, carry $300,000 of third party liability insurance. Regrettably, you cause an accident, and are punished by the courts with a $1.5 million liability payment. The insurance company is responsible only for the $300,000; that's the full extent of their commitment because that's all your premiums paid for. You, unfortunately, are on the hook for the rest ($1.2 million). Unless you have coverage for $1.5 million — or happen to be independently wealthy — you are likely to be forced to declare bankruptcy.

On its own, liability insurance provides insufficient protection. After all, in many accidents, no one individual is negligent. For example, consider a policyholder who suffers a heart attack while behind the wheel. The automobile swerves out of control, causing serious injuries to passengers in another automobile. In the ensuing legal proceeding, even if the driver who suffered the heart attack is found negligent, his property (vehicle) and his body have also suffered injury. Should he or she not be entitled to recover at least a portion of the costs? The bottom line is, even with liability insurance, other costs associated with an accident can be staggering. Because of these concerns, most provinces require that drivers also carry accident benefits insurance, which compensates parties for damages incurred *regardless of who might have been at fault.* (Note that accident benefits coverage is not mandatory in Newfoundland. And in Quebec, a government agency manages accident benefits related to bodily injury, while private insurance providers supply property damage insurance.)

Once you and the insurance company agree on how much liability and accident insurance you will purchase, and on other related details, a contract is signed. (An exception is where the provincial government supervises the insurance plan; there, no formal contract is signed.) Once the contract is signed, each party has specific obligations.

Of course, the second party (the insurance company) is obligated to pay should the first party be found negligent or if accident benefits must be paid out. But what happens if the insurance company goes bankrupt before it can pay the claim? While such bankruptcies are rare, Canadian insurance companies, in conjunction with regulatory approval, fund something called the Property and Casualty Insurance Compensation Corporation. The role of PACICC is to pay pending claims should an insurance company go bankrupt. Claims are paid up to a maximum of $250,000 or the amount of the claim, whichever is lower. In addition, 70% of the unexpired portion of the premium is refunded, up to $700 per policy.

The first party has obligations as well, such as not driving with a suspended license. If you took the risk of driving while under suspension and became involved in an accident, it's likely that the insurer would simply deny coverage, saying that you had violated the terms of the contract. If you violated the contract, then it would not be held responsible for third party compensation or accident benefits. So what would happen then?

Clearly it would be unfair to deny compensation to a third party victim simply because the first party violated the terms of the insurer's contract. In recognition of that unfairness, the concept of *absolute liability* has been introduced. Absolute liability requires insurance companies to compensate the innocent third party *even when the first party has violated the insurance contract*. So the third party is at least taken care of. The first party, alas, won't be so fortunate; he or she is required to reimburse the insurer for all the money that it paid out.

The Automobile Insurance Industry

As a general rule, firms that offer automobile insurance are large companies that also sell other types of insurance, such as home and business insurance. Firms do not typically specialize in providing automobile insurance alone; because automobile insurance is so highly regulated, it is surprisingly unprofitable. In fact, a firm might give you a discount on your car insurance just to get you to purchase other, less regulated, insurance as part of a package. Most automobile insurance is marketed by so-called property and casualty (P&C) insurance providers. According to the Insurance Bureau of Canada, more than half of all private sector insurance premiums derive from automobile insurance, generating more than $9 billion in premiums revenue annually. In addition, government-owned corporations earn an additional $4.3 billion in automobile insurance premiums.

Like its counterparts in other countries, Canada's P&C insurance industry has slowly been consolidating through mergers and acquisitions. According to the federal Department of Finance, in 1980 the 26 largest P&C providers earned half the premiums; in 1997, the top 10 firms earned half the premiums. However, no single firm controls more than 10% of the total market, which means that pricing tends to be competitive.

Table 5.2 lists the top ten property and casualty insurance providers in Canada, in terms of annual premiums. As you'll see, only three companies are Canadian; the rest are foreign-owned.

Table 5.2
Top Ten P&C Insurers in Canada, 1997

Name	Country of Origin	Net Premiums Written ($000)
General Accident Assurance Company of Canada	UK	1,430,319
Co-operators Group Limited	Canada	1,123,605
Royal & SunAlliance Canada	UK	1,118,823
ING Canada	Netherlands	1,118,610
AXA Canada Inc.	France	867,318
State Farm Insurance Companies	USA	816,549
Economical Insurance Group	Canada	686,038
Wawanesa Mutual Insurance Company	Canada	643,196
Zurich Canada	Switzerland	601,736
Liberty Mutual Group	USA	574,923

Source: *Canadian Insurance* (Ottawa: Department of Finance, 1999). Available online at http://www.fin.gc.ca/toce/1999/propertye.html

Adverse Selection and Automobile Insurance

As we explained in Chapter 1, in theory, insurance premiums should reflect the (discounted) value of the insurance benefit, adjusted for the probability that an insurance "event" might occur. In reality, asymmetric information problems between policyholders and insurance providers result in prices that divert from the theoretical present value of insurance benefits. Because the insurance company is unable to distinguish fully between high-risk and low-risk first parties, it uses generalizations to characterize policyholders. The company will charge a single premium to all first parties in a certain class, such as those in a specific age, gender, or geographical group, although the actual riskiness of individuals within the class may differ from the average of the class. Hence, low-risk first parties are overcharged when they purchase automobile insurance, while high-risk first parties are undercharged.

Because of these generalizations, more high-risk consumers within a class will purchase insurance than low-risk consumers. The disproportionate number of high-risk clients results in the insurance company's taking on more risk than initial estimates of the population would suggest, a phenomenon described in Chapter 1 as "adverse selection."

Mandatory automobile insurance works to the benefit of high-risk policyholders at the expense of low-risk drivers. After all, the insurance company gets more business than it would otherwise, while high-risk policyholders get insurance at a cheaper price than they would otherwise. At the same time, low-risk policyholders pay more for insurance than they would otherwise.

Price Dispersion in the Automobile Insurance Industry

There is significant evidence, both anecdotal and empirical, that automobile insurance prices are widely diverse. The same set of facts can generate one quote that is twice as high as another.

Consider the following scenario. You want to purchase automobile insurance. You've received driver training, have been insured for at least one year before requesting the price quote, and have managed to avoid accidents. As well, your record is untainted by traffic violations or license suspensions.

The automobile you wish to insure is a four-door Volkswagen Jetta GLS V6 purchased in 2000. You use the automobile exclusively for personal, not business use, and expect to drive an average of 11,000 kilometres a year. You reside in Toronto. How much should you pay for automobile insurance?

Using these parameters, we requested quotes from five Canadian insurers (names changed to protect the guilty) on the same day in November 2000. We assumed the standard $300 deductible collision coverage throughout. We asked the insurers to provide quotes for two prospective buyers: an 18-year-old unmarried male and a 42-year-old married female. What we found is shown in Table 5.3.

Table 5.3
Automobile Insurance Quotes, November 2000

	Premium per Year	
Company	**18-year-old Unmarried Male**	**42-year-old Married Female**
A	$8,289	$1,681
B	9,206	1,961
C	9,496	1,763
D	12,368	1,847
E	13,000	1,653

From Table 5.3 we are able to make three observations.

Observation 1: Wide Variation in Premiums

Our first observation is that insurance premiums can vary greatly. For the 18-year-old unmarried male, the premiums range from $8,289 through $13,000. This represents a difference of $4,711 between the highest and lowest quotes; the highest quote is approximately 57% more than the lowest. For the 42-year-old married female, insurance premiums range from $1,653 to $1,961. This represents a difference of $308 between the highest and the lowest quotes, and the highest quote is approximately 19% more than the lowest. How can we explain this? Why are the quotes, though based on the same parameters, so diverse?

Some theorists argue that these findings represent a *temporary disequilibrium*. According to this argument, the quotes *should* be much closer to each other, but are temporarily diverse. Over time, as insurance providers react to the prices of their competitors, the differences should shrink. In reality, however, time does not seem to bring prices closer together. This provides little support for the temporary disequilibrium argument.

Others argue that there are differences in the quality of insurance provided by each firm. One firm may pay its claims promptly, while others tie up clients in lengthy and costly litigation. One firm may rent fancy offices, while another does business through the mail. But in our example above, the same company, E Inc., posted the highest premium for one class of policyholder and the lowest premium for another class. This seems to refute the argument that price dispersion can be explained simply by differences in quality or expenses.

Others argue that price dispersion results from the failure of potential policyholders to recognize the large differences in prices that may be charged by different insurers. Because consumers are unaware that differences exist, they fail to search for the lowest price. A similar argument is that the costs associated with switching policies lead policyholders to continue to use overpriced insurance providers. These costs may include the time required to determine the best insurance product and price mix, and the effort required to figure out exactly what is being offered by each company. And even if a better price mix is found, the original contract may include clauses that impose a high cost for switching on policyholders. It's also possible that the consumer may feel a certain loyalty (possibly misplaced) to the insurance company representative, who may be a friend or relative.

The lesson to you should be crystal clear. Checking out insurance costs has substantial benefits — you should shop around each and every time your policy comes up for renewal. You will be amazed at how some companies will charge you much more than what you are currently paying and others will charge you much less. Insurance is definitely not a commodity!

Observation 2: Strategic Competition

Our second observation is that firms compete strategically for different classes of policyholders. This fact is clear from our example. For 18-year-old unmarried males, E Inc.'s premiums are the highest of the five companies. Conversely, their premiums are the lowest for 42-year-old married females. This suggests that E Inc. chooses to compete more aggressively in the middle-aged market than it does for new policyholders. A company may feel that it has a marketing advantage when dealing with one class of policyholder, and may use price competition as part of its strategy.

Observation 3: Risk Classification

The third observation we can draw is that certain classes of policyholders are classified as riskier. The average quote for the 18-year-old unmarried male is approximately $10,472, while the average quote for the 42-year old married female is approximately $1,781. The difference between the two is staggering: approximately $8,691. In other words, automobile insurance for the average 18-year-old unmarried male is almost *six times* the cost that it is for the average 42-year-old married female. Insurance companies clearly consider young unmarried males to be much riskier than middle-aged married females.

Let's explore the risk profiles associated with different age groups more closely. Table 5.4 specifies fatalities and injuries from motor vehicle accidents for each of several age groups. Insurance companies do not discriminate unfairly against young drivers. Rather, they are reacting to the probability and

Table 5.4
Fatalities and Injuries by Age Group, 1998

Age Group (years)	Fatalities	Injuries
0–4	40	3,211
5–14	119	14,605
15–19	324	28,797
20–24	381	27,934
25–34	503	42,935
35–44	437	38,129
45–54	326	26,040
55–64	233	14,161
65 +	549	15,259
Not stated	15	6,543
Total	**2,927**	**217,614**

Source: Canadian Motor Vehicle Traffic Collision Statistics, TP3322 (Ottawa: Transport Canada, October 1999). Available online at http://www.tc.gc.ca/securiteroutiere/stats/stats98/en/st98agee.htm

magnitude of future claims. As we explained in Chapter 1, it's all about probabilities and magnitudes.

Factors Affecting Automobile Insurance Premiums

As we've seen, automobile insurance contracts are not like commodities such as heating oil, where the price is identical for every unit sold. Premiums vary widely depending on the risk characteristics of drivers. By risk characteristics we don't mean just your personal propensity for risk. In other words, we are not concerned simply about aspects of your personality, such as whether you are an aggressive driver. We are referring to the risks associated with all aspects of the policy, including the nature of the contract, the type of automobile, where you drive, and other factors. Let's examine some of those factors.

Insurance premiums are positively related to the amounts the insurance company must pay out in claims against its policyholders. In other words, the more likely the policyholder is to get into an accident or have an automobile stolen, the higher the insurance premiums are likely to be. Therefore, any factors that can be used to proxy the likelihood of an accident or theft can be used as a basis on which premiums are determined. A *proxy* is a measurable variable that is used to estimate the values of a non-measurable variable — in this case, the likelihood of accident or theft. This determination takes place during the ratemaking process — the process by which insurers determine risks and pricing for insurance. Note, however, that all of these measures are based on historical data, and so do not necessarily reflect the future. After all, expectations based on history do not always reflect present reality. Still, more often than not, historical results have been found to reflect the future.

Let's look at some of the more relevant factors that proxy the likelihood of accident or theft, and that can therefore affect insurance premiums.

What type of automobile do you drive and how old is it?

Obviously, insurance premiums relate directly to the type and age of your automobile. Cheaper autos are less costly to replace, and the cost of repairing cheaper autos is typically less than the cost of repairing more expensive models. Hence, insurance premiums tend to be lower for cheaper autos. At the same time, some autos may be considered safer and less likely to be involved in accidents. Because the insurance company is less likely to pay out, premiums for such vehicles are lower.

To explore the concept further, consider the following example. Assume there are five autos, all of which initially cost $20,000. Is the insurance premium identical for all of these vehicles? Initially, you might be tempted to answer yes. After all, the autos all carry the same cost, so why not the same insurance premium?

Such an answer is, in fact, partially correct. Third party liability insurance premiums are generally unaffected by the type of automobile you drive; they depend more on the propensity of the policyholder to act negligently. But, based on our discussion, there are indeed many reasons why the insurance premiums associated with accident benefits may vary widely for different autos. The reason is that some autos are more (or less) likely to be damaged in an accident or more (or less) likely to be stolen. In Canada, the Canadian Loss Experience Automobile Rating (CLEAR) system — developed by the non-profit Vehicle Information Centre of Canada (VICC) and funded by the Canadian automobile insurance industry — ensures that insurance premiums reflect the propensity for autos to be damaged or stolen.

For this reason, price alone is not a sufficient reason for choosing one automobile over another. The prospective automobile owner or lessor must also consider the insurance premiums associated with the automobile. This information is easily accessible, as VICC publishes material that advises consumers about the impact of automobile choice on insurance premiums. (Contact information is presented at the end of this book.)

Do you use the automobile for pleasure or business?

Historical tests demonstrate that driving to work typically results in more accidents than driving for pleasure. This is because most people drive to work during rush hours, when traffic is heaviest and accidents are more likely to occur. Therefore, premiums are typically higher when you use your automobile for business purposes.

Figure 5.1 specifies the number of casualties that take place during different times of the day. It appears to support the contention that more casualties occur during rush hour, particularly in the evening rush hour.

Casualties by Time of Day, 1998

Figure 5.1

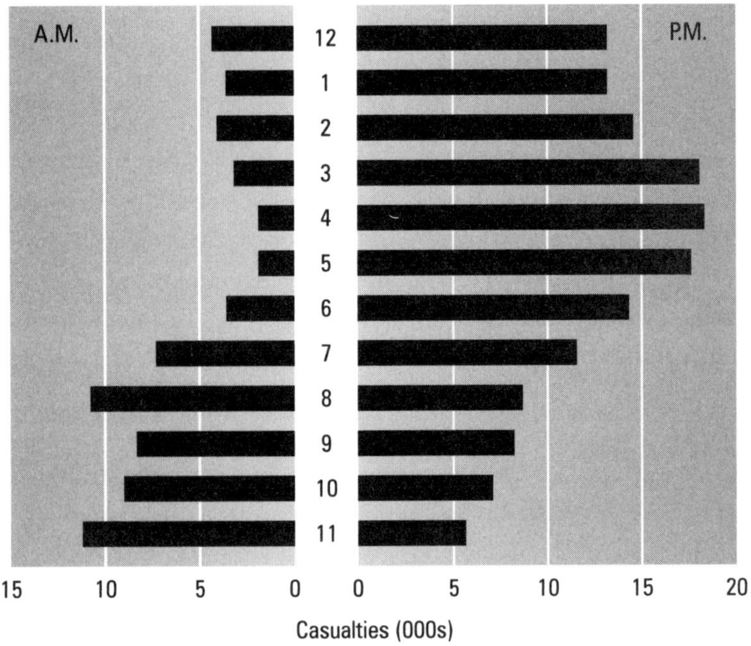

Source: Canadian Motor Vehicle Traffic Collision Statistics, TP3322 (Ottawa: Transport Canada, October 1999). Available online from www.tc.gc.ca/roadsafety/STATS/stats98/en/st98time.htm

Where do you drive?

Besides looking at driver characteristics, insurance companies will analyze the region in which the policyholder drives. Some regions, such as heavily populated urban centres, have historically experienced more accidents and automobile thefts — and consumers in those regions pay higher insurance premiums.

Table 5.5 specifies the number of casualties that occur in urban and non-urban locations. Note that in this context, "urban" refers to both metropolitan roads and streets and other urban areas, or a collision site where the speed limit is 60 kilometres per hour or less. "Rural" refers to primary and secondary highways as well as local roads, or a collision site where the speed limit exceeds 60 kilometres per hour.

Table 5.5
Traffic Collisions by Place of Occurrence, 1998

Occurrence	Urban	Rural	Not Stated
Fatality	926	1,643	23
Personal injury	103,845	40,883	3,599
Total	**104,771**	**42,526**	**3,622**

Source: 1998 Canadian Motor Vehicle Traffic Collision Statistics, TP3322 (Ottawa: Transport Canada, October 1999). Available online at: http://www.tc.gc.ca/roadsafety/STATS/stats98/en/st98cone.htm#Place

Table 5.5 goes a long way towards explaining why policy-holders living in the country tend to pay lower automobile insurance premiums than their urban counterparts. Although speeds are higher, there is much less traffic in rural areas and, hence, fewer accidents.

How much do you drive?

The more an automobile is driven, the more likely it is that it will be involved in an accident. Hence, some insurance companies charge higher premiums for more heavily driven autos.

What is your driving record?

For obvious reasons, an individual who has already committed numerous moving traffic violations is perceived as more likely to get into an accident in the future. Therefore we expect to find a positive correlation between driving records and insurance premiums. The more offences on your record, the higher your premiums are likely to be. Similarly, statistical tests demonstrate that individuals found responsible for accidents in the past, specifically in the previous three years, are more likely to cause an accident again in the future. Insurers will also look at the records of other people in the household who drive the automobile. Do they have a history of traffic violations and/or accidents? If they do, higher insurance premiums may result.

What are your age, gender, and marital status?

Based on historical data, young, unmarried males are more likely to get into accidents than any other group. Therefore, age, gender, and marital status variables are generally accepted as proxies for risk, and young, unmarried males pay higher insurance premiums than other groups.

What is the deductible?

Insurance companies charge lower premiums for contracts with larger deductibles. For example, if your deductible is $500, the insurer is responsible only for damages in excess of that amount. Because thousands of smaller accidents occur in which property damage is minimal, the deductible eliminates numerous minor accidents from the company's caseload, resulting in lower management and personnel costs. These savings, or a portion thereof, can be passed on in the form of lower premiums.

However, there is another important reason for deductibles. The deductible allows policyholders to avoid moral hazard. You will recall that moral hazard refers to situations in which an individual drives recklessly, knowing that the insurance company can't observe the driving and that he or she will not incur the cost of the reckless behaviour.

Potential reckless behaviour is restrained by the risk of large costs to the policyholder should an accident take place. These personal costs may be the physical harm the policyholder suffers, or possibly the legal and financial difficulties associated with filing a claim. While it's wrong to say that the deductible, and the deductible alone, acts to mitigate moral hazard, it is reasonable to argue that the larger the deductible, the greater the monetary costs to the policyholder should she or he behave recklessly. Hence we would expect to see a negative relationship between the cost of the deductible and reckless behaviour. So, deductibles may lower the number of accidents.

Summary Points

- The inefficiencies associated with the tort-compensation automobile insurance system have led some jurisdictions to implement a no-fault automobile insurance system. Not only does this eliminate inefficiencies such as legal costs, delays, use of public legal resources, and perceived unfair liability, it may even have medical benefits through allowing victims to avoid years of focusing on their injuries.
- Automobile insurance is mandatory, while most other insurance is not. This is because of the potential harm to strangers that a person may cause while driving, the magnitude of potential liability, and the leverage the government has over drivers through the ability to suspend driving licenses. Mandatory insurance varies from jurisdiction to jurisdiction. Throughout Canada, minimum compulsory insurance coverage typically includes third party liability coverage, statutory accident benefits, and uninsured automobile coverage. The amount and duration of the coverage vary greatly between jurisdictions.
- Most automobile insurance in Canada is marketed through property and casualty (P&C) insurance providers. More

than half of all private sector insurance premiums derive from automobile insurance. The top 10 P&C firms earned half of all premiums not received by government corporations in 1997, suggesting consolidation of the industry.

- Adverse selection is an important component of the insurance pricing game, as insurance prices are highly regulated and everyone must purchase insurance, even people who perceive it as overpriced.
- Automobile insurance prices are highly dispersed. Quotes given for the same individual, car, and plan can vary by thousands of dollars. This may be caused by temporary disequilibrium, differences in quality, consumer unwillingness to undertake qualitative searches, or firms focusing their price-competition efforts on specific segments of the population.
- Automobile insurance prices are influenced by a number of factors, including automobile model and age; purpose, location, and extent of driving; driving record; age, gender, and marital status; and deductible. Hence, insurance choices and lifestyle decisions must be made jointly in the context of these considerations.

How to Sound Intelligent

Some Questions to Ask When Purchasing Automobile Insurance

- What does my automobile insurance policy include and exclude? To whom does it apply? Where does it apply?
- What risks do I face if I purchase only mandatory insurance?
- Which optional insurance is for me?
- Which car should I purchase to minimize my automobile insurance premiums? How does CLEAR rate my car?
- How would a change in the way I travel to work affect my insurance premiums?

- How would my premiums vary for different deductibles?
- Have I researched a number of different quotes by comparison shopping among different insurance providers? Why are the premiums different?
- How flexible and understanding will each potential insurance provider be if I am found at fault in an accident or commit a moving violation? How will these events affect my premiums?
- What level of service does each potential insurance provider provide should I have to make a claim?

6

Property Insurance

Imagine the following scenario: Termites have been quietly eating away at the foundations of your house for the past 10 years. One evening, part of the foundation suddenly caves in. You and your family manage to escape the house, but as you are running out, looking over your shoulder at your dramatically collapsing house, you slam into a woman bicycling along the sidewalk, breaking both her legs.

After helping the poor woman into the ambulance, you start to think about the financial implications of your bizarre evening. Your family managed to survive uninjured, and you are thankful for that. But your house is totalled, and you are probably going to be facing a lawsuit from the injured woman — she has already called her lawyer on her cellphone!

Six months ago, you prudently purchased property insurance through your brother-in-law, the insurance agent. You've never had time to read the fine details — your brother-in-law said it was a standard contract — but it is property insurance, after all. And you just saw your home collapse. Of course, you must be covered — what could be more obvious? Now if only you had purchased insurance against the personal liability you are facing because of the injury you caused!

Guess what? In reality, that analysis of the financial implications of the evening's events is *completely wrong*. We use the above scenario to demonstrate the peculiar nature of property insurance. It covers a lot more than your home, and it does not cover your home as expansively as you might think. Your insurance company will likely pay for legal fees and the liability you face because of breaking the woman's legs. As we will discuss in this chapter, property insurance coverage protects against any personal liability you may face because of bodily injury you unintentionally inflict, anywhere in the world. But your property insurance will not protect against damage by insects. You can forget about receiving compensation for your destroyed house!

We begin this chapter by explaining exactly what property insurance is — and what it is not.

What Is Property Insurance?

Property insurance is a package of protection. Unlike automobile insurance, it is not mandatory, but it may be required in order to get financing to purchase a home. The major components of the property insurance package are as follows:

- protection against perils
  - protection against damage to the insured residence caused by a peril
  - protection against loss or damage of personal property, anywhere in the world, caused by a peril
  - protection against additional living expenses that come about because of a peril

- protection against personal legal liability
  - protection against personal legal liability for unintentionally causing bodily injuries or property damage to others
  - other "voluntary" payments and compensation, even when the policyholder is not at fault

Note that the property insurance policy does not cover damage or liability associated with a home-based business. To protect a home-based business, an *endorsement* (an extension of the policy) to the property insurance or a separate policy must be acquired. As well, note that some households, such as those of tenants and condominium owners, do not require all the components of the property insurance package we've described. We discuss these households later on in this chapter.

Let's explore the components of the property insurance package — protection against perils and against personal legal liability — in detail.

Which Perils Are Covered?

Which perils — events that can cause a loss — are covered in the property insurance contract? That depends on the type of coverage. Property insurance coverage has three broad categories: basic, comprehensive, and broad.

The most restrictive — and least expensive — coverage is provided in a basic policy, which provides coverage for damage to the insured residence and personal property caused by specific perils. It is often referred to as *named perils* coverage. The named perils typically include fire, lightning, explosion, electric current, falling objects, impact by aircraft or land vehicles, riot, transportation of property, water damage, smoke, windstorm or hail, vandalism or malicious acts, and burglary. However, not all damage is covered within the above categories. For example, although water damage is covered, water damage caused by repeated water seepage or malfunctioning sump pumps is excluded, as are some other causes of water damage. As another example, smoke damage does not include smoke from fireplaces.

The most liberal — and most expensive — coverage is provided by *comprehensive* property insurance. Sometimes called *all risks* coverage, it provides coverage for damage to the insured residence and personal property caused by all perils not specifically excluded in the policy. However, many perils *are* excluded, hence the term "all risks" is misleading. For example, a comprehensive policy may cover paint spills on furniture but explicitly exclude coverage for earthquakes, furnace oil spills, and sewer backups. However, optional coverage can be purchased for these perils as well, for additional premiums.

The *broad* policy is a compromise between the comprehensive and basic policies. On one hand, loss or damage of personal property is covered only if it is caused by perils specified in the more restrictive basic policy. On the other hand, damage to the insured residence is covered using the more liberal specification of perils from the comprehensive policy. The broad policy thus provides stronger protection for the residence, damage to which can be much more costly than damage to property.

Why are insurance companies so careful when defining the perils for which they provide protection? There are three reasons why many perils are not covered. First, the more perils covered, the greater the risk the insurance company faces, and the higher the premiums. Hence, limiting the perils that are covered effectively lowers the cost of insurance, thereby increasing consumer demand. Second, insurance companies do not want policyholders to use the property insurance contract as an elaborate (and costly) maintenance contract. The more preventable an event, the less need there is for insurance. Hence, if the peril is preventable — for example, the termite damage in the scenario discussed earlier — the insurance company will exclude it from the policy. Third, insurance companies do not wish to insure against the inevitable. Hence, if you live on a flood plain, flooding will not be covered. The insurance company won't shovel your snow after winter snowstorms either!

But why not allow households to insure against preventable and inevitable perils? The answer lies in the concepts of moral hazard and adverse selection discussed in Chapters 2 and 3. While moral hazard and adverse selection issues exist for all aspects of property insurance, they are more acute for preventable and inevitable perils. With preventable perils, policyholders face moral hazard; they may avoid making necessary repairs, knowing that the insurance company can't observe their behaviour. Adverse selection occurs with both preventable and inevitable perils, as the policyholder may have private information regarding the real likelihood of making a future claim. People who have such private information, and thus have a higher probability of making a future claim, are more likely to purchase property insurance.

The amount of compensation received will depend on the deductible chosen. As discussed earlier, the higher the deductible, the lower the insurance premiums. This makes sense, as a higher deductible effectively lowers the number of small, yet administratively costly claims against the insurance company. Hence, one reason to consider a higher deductible is the associated lower premiums. Another reason to consider a higher deductible is that it will effectively change your behaviour — a higher deductible means you will make fewer claims. As we will discuss later in this chapter, it's in the policyholder's best interest to limit the number of claims made.

Protection Against Damage to the Insured Residence

What is the value of the compensation that the insurance company provides if the insured residence is damaged because of a peril? The maximum amount of compensation is specified when the contract is signed. The general approach is to appraise the value of replacing the home — not its market value — and to determine the percentage of the replacement value to cover, typically more than 80%.

But there are two dangers inherent in this process. First, 80% coverage may sound sufficient before damage occurs, but consider a situation in which your house is destroyed by a fire. If it costs $250,000 to replace your home (including removing the remnants of your destroyed house), 80% coverage will leave you $50,000 short — a significant financial burden! Second, the appraisal may underestimate the true replacement cost. Therefore, even if you think you are fully covered, you may end up facing a heavy financial burden if the amount of coverage specified in the policy is too conservative.

Another type of coverage, designated *guaranteed replacement cost* coverage, will make up the shortfall between 100% coverage and the actual cost of replacing the home. The insurance company must be informed of any renovations to the home — such as a new kitchen — because the change in replacement value caused by these renovations will influence the value of the guaranteed replacement cost coverage, as well as the premiums. Even with guaranteed replacement cost coverage, the insurance company will not pay for the new building to comply with recent changes in construction codes and zoning bylaws. An optional endorsement can be purchased to cover risks associated with bylaw changes.

Other structures at the same location as the insured residence — for example, a detached garage or garden shed — are typically insured for up to 10% of the coverage on the insured residence. As well, plants (but not lawns) are typically covered for up to 5% of the coverage on the insured residence, to a specified maximum. Other dwellings that you own, such as a cottage, are not covered, but can be insured separately or added to the existing property insurance policy. If they are insured separately, you do not require the personal legal liability coverage, which you already get from your main coverage. Large boats and some other unlicensed motorized vehicles, such as off-road recreational vehicles, must be insured separately as well.

Protection Against Loss or Damage of Personal Property

The perils covered, the amount of coverage, and the location of coverage are all aspects of protection against loss or damage of personal property. As we discussed earlier, the perils covered will depend on the type of policy. A comprehensive policy will cover damage to personal property caused by any peril not specifically excluded in the policy, while the basic and broad policies will cover loss or damage caused by named perils. The amount of coverage for personal property is typically specified as a percentage (for example, 70%) of the insured residence value. For tenants and condominium owners, who are discussed later, the value of the insured belongings is estimated.

Specific limits are set for some personal property claims. There may be limits to coverage (for example, $10,000) for property damaged while in possession of a member of the household anywhere in the world. There are also limits for theft or burglary from an automobile, for property of a student studying away from home, and for uninsured property owned by someone else (excluding tenants or boarders) that is damaged in your home by a peril.

Specific limits are also set for certain types of personal property. For example, the policy will likely specify a limit for small watercraft or computer software. For other types of personal property, limits to coverage may apply if the property is lost or stolen or mysteriously disappears. It's clearly important to read the fine print of your policy — your coverage may be insufficient for that $10,000 gold watch! With some exceptions, you will be able to add an endorsement for specific valuables such as jewellery, watches, furs, manuscripts, guns, and bicycles. To do so, you must schedule (list) the valuables and the amount for which they are insured, which is often based on an appraisal. This will be expensive in terms of premiums, but may be the only way to insure some valuables.

When you make a claim, the insurance company will replace the damaged property or may be willing to agree to a cash settlement. Superficially, a cash settlement may sound ideal. For example, you don't do much stargazing anymore, so you'd rather get the cash than replace that $4,000 telescope. However, cash settlements are for the "actual cash value" of the lost or damaged property. This means that the insurance company will pay the value of the damaged property minus an amount for appraised *depreciation* — loss of value caused by physical deterioration or obsolescence. The rationale behind using actual cash value as the basis for cash settlements is obvious. Without it, some people might be motivated to fraudulently destroy their property in order to get their hands on the money. With actual cash value as the basis for settlements, an individual is unlikely to get more cash by fraudulently destroying his or her property than by selling it. We discuss fraud and fraudsters (people who perpetrate fraud) extensively in Chapter 8.

Protection Against Additional Living Expenses

As a supplement to the compensation provided for damage to the insured residence and personal property, the property insurance policy also provides compensation for additional living expenses, including moving expenses, that are incurred because of the damage. The compensation is received if the home is declared unfit to live in or if the household is denied access to the home, which might occur because of a peril (for example, a gas leak) occurring in the neighbourhood. As well, if you share your home with tenants, the policy will provide compensation equivalent to the "fair rental value" of the part that you rent out.

The objective of the additional living expenses payments is to permit the household to maintain the standard of living it had before occurrence of the damage, at the same cost as before the damage occurred. If you temporarily move to a hotel 20 kilometres from your home, not only will the insurance company pay for your meals and accommodation, it will pay for additional transportation costs to and from work. But it will not cover your mortgage payments or your regular, pre-damage transportation costs, as those would have been incurred whether or not the damage had taken place. The single claim limit is typically 20% of the coverage for the insured residence. And compensation is not open-ended; the insurance company limits it to the shortest amount of time reasonably required to repair the damage or to relocate permanently.

Protection Against Personal Legal Liability

The property insurance package provides protection for members of your household against legal liability for unintentionally caused bodily injuries or property damage to others. As we discussed extensively in Chapter 5, legal liability comes about when an individual (the first party) causes loss to another party (the third party) because of negligence. While legal liability protection is sold as part of the property insurance package, it does not apply exclusively to bodily injuries or property damage that occurs on the insured property. Rather, the protection covers personal legal liability you may face *anywhere in the world*. Whether a guest trips over a loose floorboard in your home or you injure someone while in-line skating in Manhattan, you are protected against personal legal liability.

In Chapter 5 we presented an argument in the context of automobile insurance that society might be better off not permitting drivers to acquire liability insurance. Society makes us legally liable for our actions for two reasons: to motivate us to avoid actions that may result in liability, and to compensate the victims of our actions. If we hold liability insurance, our motivation to avoid actions that may result in legal liability is lessened. One of the counter-arguments presented in Chapter 5 is that the bodily injury a driver may face provides sufficient motivation to avoid accidents. Will this argument hold in the context of property insurance? We believe so. After all, if a guest can trip over that loose floorboard or slip on a wet floor, so can you and your family. The fear of bodily injury will compel you to maintain a safe home, regardless of any legal liability you might face.

Of course, regardless of the risk, some households will not maintain a safe home. For example, everyone in your household may be so familiar with that hole in the backyard that they face no real danger — but your guest's dog has just disappeared down it! Or the owner of a residence may not actually live there, and therefore risks no personal harm. For such scenarios, fear of bodily injury does not motivate behaviour. But in Chapter 5 we discussed a number of other compelling arguments as to why insurance is good for society, particularly how it ensures that injured third parties — the victims — receive compensation.

Unlike the protection associated with perils, no deductibles are associated with the personal liability insurance portion of the property insurance package. As well, legal defence costs are covered beyond policy limits. However, you may not necessarily be able to use your own lawyer; your insurance company may choose who will represent you. The insurance company will provide legal defence costs if you are sued for injuring another party's body or property, regardless of the outcome, but they have the right to settle the lawsuit as they wish.

There are limits to personal liability coverage. First, and most important, the damage must be caused by an unintentional incident and must be unrelated to business. If you get in a fight and injure someone, or break one too many dishes while celebrating at a Greek restaurant, don't expect your insurance company to come to your rescue. You are also not covered for the results of physical or sexual abuse, or for transmitting a disease, even unintentionally.

Second, you are covered only for compensatory damages, not for punitive damages, even when the incident was unintentional. *Compensatory damages* are funds awarded to the third party to reimburse the actual costs associated with the incident, such as lost wages or medical bills. They also provide compensation for difficult-to-measure effects, such as pain and suffering. *Punitive damages* are funds awarded to the third party to punish the first party and to deter both the third party and others from similar conduct.

Personal legal liability coverage provides protection for a number of other circumstances. These include legal liability associated with portions of your home that you rent to others, within certain constraints. As well, it applies to trailers (when detached from a motor vehicle), small boats, golf carts, lawnmowers, snow blowers, garden tractors, and motorized wheelchairs. Further, the coverage applies to the non-business, non-racing use of unlicensed motorized vehicles, such as watercraft and off-road vehicles, *not owned* by the insured household.

This coverage applies only to liability, not to damage of the unlicensed motorized vehicles.

As we've demonstrated, the personal legal liability portion of a property insurance policy provides coverage for a wide number of scenarios. While this is comforting, don't wait until an incident occurs to find out what you are covered for. Read the fine print of the policy carefully; you may prevent some nasty surprises later on.

Other Voluntary Payments and Compensation

In addition to protection against lawsuits and compensatory damages arising from legal liability, the property insurance policy will also specify other "voluntary" payments and compensation, even when the policyholder is not legally liable. These voluntary payments are very small, but permit a symbolic gesture in incidents for which the policyholder may feel at least morally liable, if not legally. For example, if a child in your household (12 years old or under) intentionally damages another party's property, the voluntary payment will be the lowest of some amount (such as $1,000), the actual cash value, or the replacement costs. As another example, the insurance company may pay a limited amount of voluntary compensation to employees of your residence who are injured or accidentally killed while working in the residence, but conditional on the employee or the beneficiary signing a release giving up any right to sue you.

Property Insurance for Tenants and Condominium Owners

Some households do not require all the components of the property insurance package we've described. Two such households are those of tenants and condominium owners. If you rent your residence, you don't need protection against damage to the insured residence caused by a peril. But you do need insurance for your personal property and protection against personal liability.

Tenant insurance is designed to include only the components of the insurance package that tenants need — hence it excludes protection against damage to the insured residence. Coverage can also be purchased for *tenant's improvements* in order to cover significant improvements the tenant may have made to the residence.

Unfortunately, some tenants do not consider property insurance necessary. This attitude may stem from a combination of causes. First, tenants tend to underestimate the value of their personal property, unlike homeowners, who also have possible damage to their residence to consider. Second, tenants tend to forget about the additional living expenses they could incur if their residence should be damaged. Third, tenants fail to recognize the personal liability they could face. If a fire starts in their rental unit that results in damage to the apartment complex, they might be found legally liable. Without liability insurance, the liability and legal costs would, in most cases, result in bankruptcy. Fourth, tenants don't require financing — they don't have a mortgage — hence, property insurance is not mandatory. This may lead some to believe that property insurance is not necessary when renting.

Condominium insurance plays a role similar to tenant insurance. The condominium corporation holds a "master policy," which covers damage to the entire structure. This includes each unit plus the common areas, such as the swimming pool, game room, and lobby. Hence, as with tenant insurance, the condominium owner does not require protection against damage to the insured residence, but does require a policy consisting of the other components of the property insurance package.

The condominium insurance policyholder may wish to acquire owner's improvements coverage, loss assessment coverage, and supplemental coverage. *Owner's improvements* coverage protects significant improvements made to the unit. *Loss assessment* coverage provides protection against certain types of special assessments related to the condominium corporation's master policy, but not against an assessment to pay a deductible in the master policy or to maintain the condominium. Loss assessment coverage does provide protection against special assessments based on legal liability or direct loss caused by an insured peril. In either case, the special assessment must be associated with a shared part of the condominium for which the master policy does not have sufficient coverage. *Supplemental* coverage protects you if the condominium corporation's master policy does not fully protect your unit.

Factors Affecting Property Insurance Premiums

The property insurance industry is quite efficient at specifying premiums in relation to future claims. To demonstrate, we use data provided by the Insurance Bureau of Canada to calculate the ratio of personal property insurance claims to net written premiums. We find that it hovers around 65%. In other words, for every $100 in personal property insurance premiums received, $65 is paid out to satisfy claims. During the period between 1984 and 1997, the ratio ranged from approximately 57% to 77%. Of course, the 35% not paid out in claims is not pure profit margin. The majority goes towards fees, commissions, management, and infrastructure expenses that the insurance company faces.

The values of claims and net written premiums for each year are presented in Figure 6.1. The ratio of personal property insurance claims to net written premiums is presented in Figure 6.2.

Net Property Insurance Premiums and Claims, 1984–97

Figure 6.1

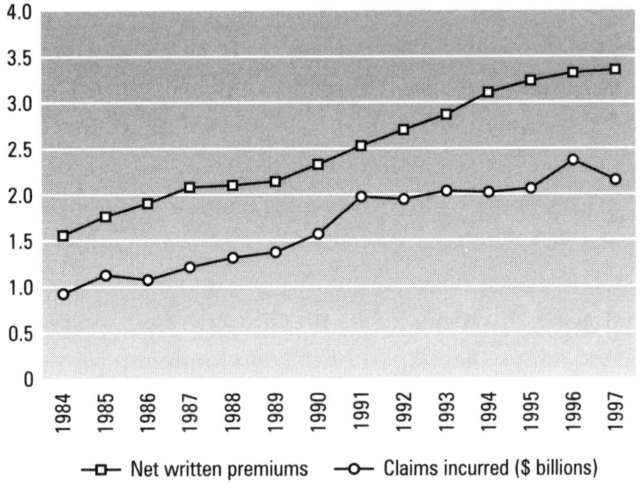

Ratio of Property Insurance Claims to Premiums, 1984–97

Figure 6.2

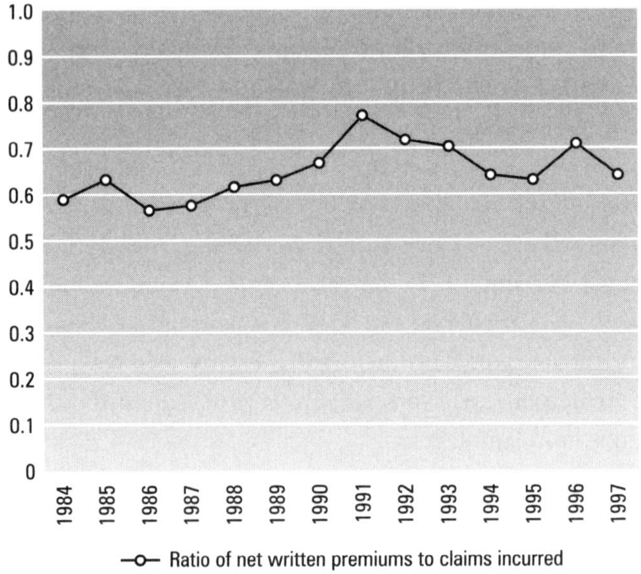

Property insurance companies aim for a ratio of personal property insurance claims to net written premiums of approximately 65%, and they have generally been successful in setting premiums that enable them to do so. This success comes from careful determination of the relationship between the types of perils, policyholders, and properties they are insuring and the associated likelihood and magnitude of future claims. This determination takes place during the ratemaking process, the process through which insurers determine risks and pricing.

As we discussed in Chapter 5, premiums depend on risk characteristics — the risks associated with all aspects of the policy. For property insurance, risk characteristics include the nature of the contract, the likelihood and magnitude of households in the geographic region facing perils, the household's claims history, and the nature of the house. While this sounds complicated (it is), the underlying principle behind determining premiums is straightforward: Identify factors that proxy the likelihood and magnitude of damage, and use them to relate premiums to households. The proxy — the measurable variable used to estimate the value of a non-measurable variable — is in this case the likelihood and magnitude of damage. If the factors suggest that the household under evaluation is more likely to result in higher claims against the insurance company, higher premiums will be charged.

Let's consider some of the major factors that proxy the likelihood and magnitude of future personal property insurance claims.

What is the probability of a peril occurring?

The more likely a peril is to occur in your region, the higher the premiums will be. And perils do vary from region to region. For example, consider Figure 6.3, which presents the number of offences for two types of property crimes — breaking and entering and theft — in British Columbia, Ontario, and Quebec in the year 2000.

Property Crimes in Three Provinces, 2000

Figure 6.3

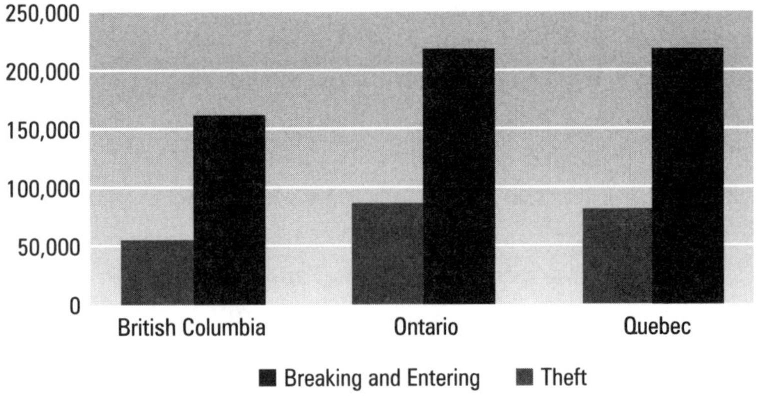

Source: Statistics Canada

Figure 6.3 suggests that residents of Ontario experience the most of either type of property crime, while Quebec and British Columbia rank second for breaking and entering and theft, respectively. However, the figure is misleading; when determining the likelihood of a peril occurring, we must consider the *per household* likelihood of the event. Using census data from 1996, we determined the per household likelihood of each crime occurring, which is presented in Figure 6.4 on the next page.

Figure 6.4 suggests that while there are more breaking and entering and theft offences in Ontario, households in British Columbia are more likely on a per household basis to experience either type of property crime. Quebec and Ontario now rank second for breaking and entering and theft, respectively.

Per Household Property Crimes in Three Provinces, 2000

Figure 6.4

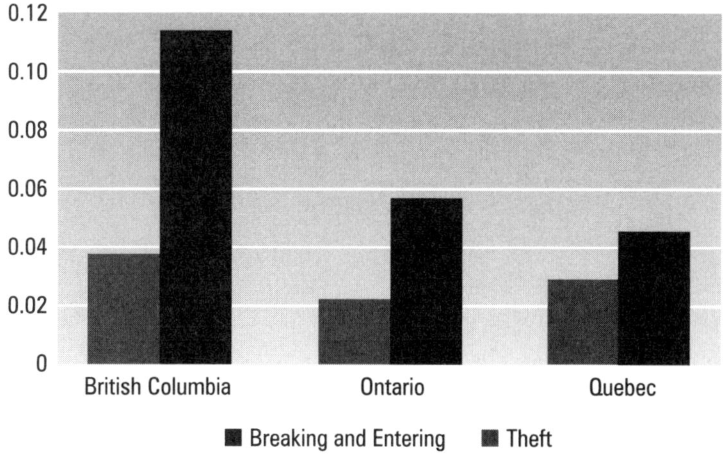

Source: Statistics Canada

What is the expected magnitude of claims?

The amount that the insurance company must pay out to satisfy claims is a function of both the probability and the magnitude of damage caused by the peril. The magnitude of the damage will depend on preventive measures in place and whether an infrastructure exists to deal with the peril. Premiums will be lower if the insured residence has preventive measures such as a burglar and fire alarm system. In terms of infrastructure, premiums will be lower if the home is in close proximity — say, eight kilometres — to a fire hall.

In a similar vein, the age of the home and the type of construction will influence premiums as well. Newer homes may receive a discount on premiums, and the insurance company may provide only limited coverage — or no coverage at all — for very old homes. Similarly, a frame house will likely cost more to insure than a brick house, as we know from the story of the three little pigs!

The issue of magnitude can be applied to liability as well. Premiums are related positively to the willingness of the liability system to award large compensatory damages. As an example, we can contrast the Canadian and U.S. liability systems. Since the U.S. liability system tends to award much larger amounts, determining Canadian premiums on the basis of a combined U.S.–Canada liability history would result in overestimated premiums for Canadians.

How many claims has the household made?

It makes intuitive sense that the more claims a household has made in the past, the higher the premiums the household will pay in the future. After all, if a household has made seven claims in the past three years, this is a good indication that future claims will take place as well. What may be less intuitive is that it's not so much the *size* of the claims as the *number* of claims that matters. Insurance companies are concerned about your household's tendency to engage in behaviour that leads to claims. So a claim is a bad signal, even if the compensation doesn't amount to much. Whenever possible, avoid making small claims. In extreme cases, too many claims may result in the insurance company deciding not to renew the policy.

What are the coverage and deductible?

The more coverage you acquire, the higher the premiums. Hence, when choosing property insurance, it's important to be careful not to overestimate and over-insure. After all, the amount that you actually receive will depend on the cost of replacement, regardless of the specified maximum.

With regard to the deductible, there are a number of reasons why a higher deductible will result in lower premiums. As we discussed earlier, larger deductibles mean that the insurance company is not obligated to satisfy numerous small, yet administratively costly, claims. As well, choosing a larger deductible allows the policyholder to avoid moral hazard, because it makes a claim costly to the policyholder as well. As discussed earlier, specifying a large deductible discourages the policyholder from making claims for incidents that result in minor damage. This leads to fewer small claims that could cause the insurance company to think of the policyholder as high-risk — without much financial benefit. In practical terms, if you don't intend to make small claims and you can afford to forgo compensation on them, you are well-advised to choose a large deductible.

In addition to the factors discussed above, you may be able to receive a discount on your property insurance by purchasing it together with your automobile insurance. Also, note that premiums are unrelated to the market value of the property. This makes sense, as the policy obligates replacement costs or actual cash value as the basis for determining compensation, both of which are independent of market value.

Summary Points

- Property insurance is a package of protection against perils and personal legal liability. Protection against perils includes protection against damage to the insured residence, loss or damage of personal property anywhere in the world, and additional living expenses. Protection against personal liability includes protection against legal liability for unintentionally causing bodily injury or property damage, as well as other "voluntary" payments and compensation.
- The three broad categories of property insurance coverage are basic, comprehensive, and broad. Basic coverage provides protection against specifically named perils. Comprehensive coverage provides protection against all perils not specifically excluded in the policy. Broad coverage provides basic-type coverage for personal property and

comprehensive-type coverage for the insured residence.

- Many perils are not covered in order to lower both the insurance company's risk and the premiums. As well, limiting the perils covered enables the insurance company to avoid insuring against preventable or inevitable perils caused by associated moral hazard and adverse selection.
- Some households, such as those of tenants and condominium owners, do not require all the components of the property insurance package. Tenant and condominium insurance are often perceived as unnecessary because the value of personal property may be underestimated; additional living expenses, should a peril occur, are not considered; personal liability is ignored; and insurance is not mandated by a mortgage provider.
- The ratio of personal property insurance claims to net written premiums in Canada hovers around 65%. Factors influencing property insurance premiums include the probability of a peril occurring in the household's geographic area, the expected magnitude of incurred claims, the number of claims the household has made, and the level of coverage and deductible.

How to Sound Intelligent

Some Questions to Ask When Purchasing Property Insurance

- Is the insurance I am purchasing appropriate for the type of dwelling my household lives in?
- Have I purchased separate insurance for my home-based business?
- Should I choose basic, comprehensive, or broad coverage?
- How much coverage should I purchase?
- Are my estimates of property value accurate?
- How large a deductible should I choose?
- Should I purchase guaranteed replacement cost coverage?

- Have I insured my cottage, other dwellings, and unlicensed motorized vehicles?
- What limits are specified in the insurance contract?
- Which valuables should I schedule?

7

Dealing with Your Insurance Company

Most of this book so far has dealt with the details of insurance contracts, such as what's covered, what's not, and the size of deductibles. In this chapter we explore characteristics of the insurance contract that are *not* in the contract's fine print, but which may play an equally important role in determining whether you are successful when you make a claim. From choosing the insurance company initially through to making a claim, failure to recognize the rules by which the insurance industry plays can be costly.

Insurance providers work hard to develop a specific public image. They want to appear reliable, traditional, and trustworthy. To sum it up in a single sentence, the insurance industry's message is "We will always be there, and we will always do as we promise." This message is important because of the nature of the relationship between insurance provider and policyholder. The insurance policy is a long-term contract based on trust. Policyholders pay premiums to their insurance companies over a long period of time, with the expectation (or hope) that the companies will provide the promised benefits when they make a claim in the future. Hence, there are two dimensions to the insurance provider's reputation in the eyes of the policyholder: the degree to which it actually satisfies claims as promised, and the probability of its failing before the claim is ever made.

Before we consider each of these dimensions in detail, remember that the reputation of the insurance company can play a significant role in the premiums that it charges. Unfortunately, some consumers make the serious mistake of choosing insurance on the basis of premiums alone. Consider the following situation. You have to purchase property insurance. You've narrowed your choice down to one of two policies. The policies are identical, but the premiums charged by one company are 75% of the premiums charged by the other. Your natural instinct is to choose the cheaper policy — and indeed, you may have found a great deal. However, the disparity between the premiums may be the result of more than your good luck. One company may be increasing its customer base by providing consumers with low premiums, while the other may compete on the basis of superior customer service. Alternatively, one company may have a much greater probability of going bankrupt within the next 10 years, while the other is financially healthy. The lesson for the consumer is, even if policies look identical in terms of the benefits they offer, there may be wide differences that you won't find out about until you make a claim.

Let's take a detailed look at the two dimensions that can determine an insurance provider's reputation.

Will the Insurance Company Satisfy Claims as Promised?

The first dimension — the degree to which the insurance company actually satisfies claims as promised — is measured by the insurance provider's behaviour when a claim is made. Is the company flexible when dealing with a claim, or will it try to find any excuse not to pay the promised benefits? Will the policyholder have to choose between dragging the insurance company through the court system or relinquishing his rightful benefits? As well, what kind of customer service is provided? Will the policyholder easily be able to contact a representative of the company, or have to wait until the end of a long weekend to speak to a human being, and then wait two months to find out if she is covered?

Differences in the behaviour of insurance companies after an incident may appear minor when you are signing a contract, but they can have serious financial implications when it comes time to make a claim. While it's often difficult to determine the true level of customer service, you should attempt to investigate each insurance provider's service policies. This can be done formally, by asking your representative to get the information directly from the company. But you can also ask your friends and relatives about their experiences with their insurance companies. When a claim was made, how did the company behave? Did they delay payment? Did they cause undue hassles? Or were they quick to resolve the claim? You may discover that the claims process of the insurance company you're considering takes three months, as opposed to other providers whose claims processes take half that time.

Aside from the above, other issues that should be taken into consideration are the provider's renewability policy, how easily your policy can be cancelled, the provider's management philosophy, the length of time the company has been in business, and the length of time the company has been offering that particular policy or similar policies.

Good customer service is not only good for consumers, it's good for the insurance company as well. Some researchers estimate that only about 15% of all consumers choose insurance on the basis of price alone, while the rest consider the insurance company's reputation as well. Evidence suggests that there is a direct link between customer service and market share: High-quality service is associated with a 6% growth in market share, while low-quality service is associated with a 2% decline in market share.[24]

A remarkable study measured customers' satisfaction with their insurance companies after a specific catastrophe, the disastrous Hurricane Hugo that struck South Carolina in 1989.[25] Researchers tested whether certain factors influenced policyholders' perception of insurance company effectiveness when they were dealing with claims in the aftermath of the storm. Not surprisingly, the study found that the shorter the insurance company's response time, the more positive the perception of its effectiveness. As well, the more adjustors or insurance company representatives involved in settling the claim, and the longer the time until the initial settlement, the more negative the perception.

Interestingly, several factors that influenced policyholders' perception of insurance company effectiveness were unrelated to the insurance company's behaviour. The researchers found that the more the policyholder knew about his or her coverage before the disaster, and the fewer insurers the policyholder had, the more positive was the perception of insurance company effectiveness. The more damage a policyholder suffered and the greater the amount of uninsured loss, the more negative the perception. These findings suggest that, regardless of effort, an insurance company may be perceived as ineffective because of a

24 Based on the Profit Impact of Marketing Strategy database in M. Drexler and T. Reedy, "Managing Customers' Profitability," *Canadian Insurance* (July 1999), 26.

25 D. P. Moore and J. W. Moore, "Insurance Company Effectiveness Under Extreme Conditions," *Group and Organization Management* 20:3 (1995), 335–80.

feeling of "sour grapes" on the part of the policyholder. This idea is reinforced by the fact that those with more damage and higher uninsured losses had the most negative perceptions.

Is the Insurance Company Likely to Fail?

The second dimension of an insurance provider's reputation is related to the probability of its failing before the claim is made. Regardless of how flexible and oriented to customer service the insurance provider tries to be, it will be unable to keep its promises if it becomes insolvent. While "insurance for insurance companies" does exist (offering limited protection, as we discuss later in this chapter), the financial health of the insurance provider plays an important role in determining its reputation.

Consumers' willingness to sign insurance contracts is greatly reduced if they perceive even the slightest likelihood that the insurance company will be unable to meet its financial obligations to policyholders. However, as we know, all private corporations face some probability of default. One's choice of insurance company cannot thus be made without consideration of its financial strength.

What factors influence the likelihood of an insurance company defaulting? To answer this question, let's look at the methodology that one organization uses. The A. M. Best Company provides independent ratings of insurance companies, including those that sell insurance in Canada. One of a number of ratings they provide is their financial strength ratings. The ratings, as illustrated in Table 7.1, are divided into two categories, *secure* and *vulnerable*.

The first category of financial strength ratings is the secure ratings, which range from a high of A++ (superior) to a low of B+ (very good). In general, an insurance company with a secure rating is considered to have a "strong or good ability to meet

Table 7.1
A. M. Best Company Financial Strength Ratings

Secure Ratings	
A++ and A+	Superior
A and A–	Excellent
B++ and B+	Very good

Vulnerable Ratings	
B and B–	Fair
C++ and C+	Marginal
C and C–	Weak
D	Poor
E	Under regulatory supervision
F	In liquidation
S	Suspended

Source: A. M. Best Co. Web site, http://www.ambest.com/ratings/ambover.pdf

their long-term obligations to members and policyholders." The second category is the vulnerable ratings, which range from a high of B (fair) to S (suspended). An insurance company with a vulnerable rating is considered to "present progressively higher risks." The probability of a secure insurance company failing to meet its obligations is much lower than the probability of a vulnerable company failing to meet its obligations.

How is an insurance company's rating determined? It's a complex process, using numerous quantitative and qualitative factors. Three types of factors are financial strength, operating performance, and market profile. Financial strength factors measure the company's balance sheet strength and its ability to meet its debt obligations. To determine financial strength, the relationship between the firm's debt and assets is analyzed, as well as other factors, such as the effect of holding companies on the organization's financial strength.

Operating performance factors measure the company's ability to generate income, so profitability and revenues are analyzed. Management's ability, which includes experience, competence, and integrity, is also evaluated. Market profile factors measure the company's ability to maintain a competitive advantage in the industry. To determine market profile, the company's market risk, event risk, and competitive market position are analyzed. The composition and mix of the company's business (for example, the geographic location of customers) is also evaluated. This makes sense; after all, if the company has customers in numerous geographic locations, a single localized catastrophe — such as the 1998 ice storm in Quebec and eastern Ontario — has less of an impact on the bottom line than for a company that has all its customers in one region.

Let's take a look at how insurance companies rate for two categories of insurance: life and health (L&H) and property and casualty (P&C). A. M. Best provides a financial strength rating for 870 L&H companies that sell insurance products in a number of countries, including Canada. The vast majority (90%) received a secure rating, while 10% received a vulnerable rating. Figure 7.1 graphs the distribution of ratings for L&H insurance companies. (These figures exclude insurance companies for which A. M. Best does not have enough information to determine a financial strength rating, such as very small firms.)

A similar distribution of ratings is found for P&C insurance companies. A. M. Best provides a financial strength rating for 2,103 P&C companies. As with the L&H companies, the vast majority (93%) received a secure rating, while 7% received a vulnerable rating. Figure 7.2 graphs the distribution of ratings for the P&C insurance companies.

Financial Strength Ratings for L&H Insurance Companies, July 18, 2000

Figure 7.1

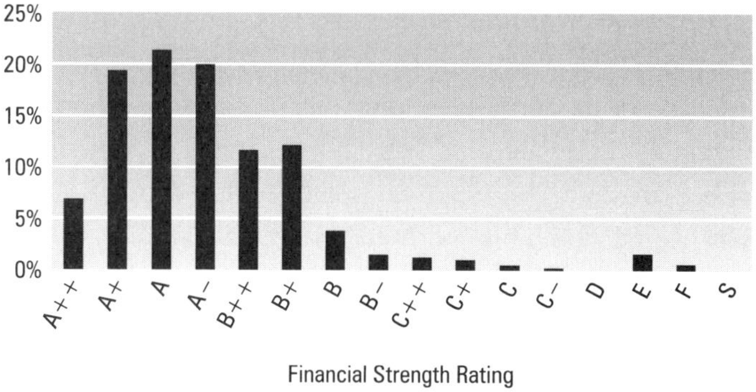

Source: A. M. Best Company, 2001

Financial Strength Ratings for P&C Insurance Companies, July 21, 2000

Figure 7.2

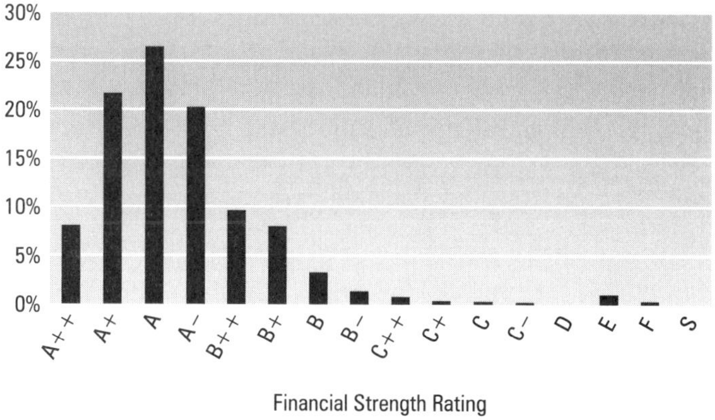

Source: A. M. Best Company, 2001

Let's consider a specific example. Clarica Life Insurance Company, formally Mutual Life of Canada, is based in Ontario. It has millions of customers in Canada, and collects billions of dollars in premiums. Its financial strength rating is A+, the second-highest possible rating. As indicated in Table 7.1, not only is an A+ rating secure, it also suggests that Clarica is "superior" in terms of financial strength, operating performance, and market profile.

Clarica has been around since 1870. However, having been around for quite some time does not necessarily mean that a company is financially strong. For example, Confederation Life, a Canadian insurance company founded in 1871, went bankrupt in 1994. This followed heavy real estate investments by the company in the 1980s, a market that collapsed in the early 1990s. The exact reasons behind the bankruptcy (and the role played by the policies of the Office of the Superintendent of Financial Institutions) are still being debated today. However, one observation is certain — those who based their trust in Confederation Life on its having been around for quite some time were sorely disappointed.

But can a rating really predict future failure? Evidence suggests that it can. According to A. M. Best, of those insurance companies rated secure three years earlier, 0.21% (approximately 1 out of 476) became insolvent. However, of those insurance companies rated vulnerable three years earlier, 2.22% (approximately 1 out of 45) became insolvent. The evidence also suggests that the different ratings within the secure and vulnerable categories are predictive as well. For example, within the secure category, of those companies rated A++ or A+ three years earlier, 0.02% (approximately 1 out of 5,000) became insolvent. At the same time, of companies rated B++ or B+, 0.5% (approximately 1 out of 200) became insolvent. As we can see, the ratings can predict to some extent the outcome of the implicit wager we make on the company's future solvency when we purchase an insurance policy.

What Happens if My Insurance Company Fails?

What happens if you made the mistake of basing your policy purchase decision on price, and not on the insurance company's reputation? Or what if you were careful to choose a highly rated company, but it happened to be the 1 in 5,000 at its rating level that went insolvent? As mentioned earlier, there is "insurance for insurance companies" that provides limited protection should your insurance company fail. The keyword here is "limited," as this insurance does not provide the exact protection your policy specifies.

Here are some details. The Property and Casualty Insurance Compensation Corporation (PACICC) provides protection should your P&C insurance company fail. Member companies from the P&C insurance industry fund PACICC. When a company fails, PACICC opens up a 45-day window of time during which it assumes that the policyholders will find alternative coverage. During this window of time, PACICC will accept claims if other sources of insurance are exhausted. It also provides a refund of 70% of "unearned" premiums — premiums paid before company failure but applicable to the time period following company failure. Should the company's liquidator reimburse you later on, the funds received from PACICC must be repaid.

PACICC is an important resource for policyholders. Not only does it insure against failure, it provides payments without delay, unlike reimbursement from the insurance company's liquidator, which could take a long time. However, PACICC has its limitations. It will not pay more than $250,000 for a single claim or to provide a refund of more than $700 in premiums. While $250,000 may sound generous, should a catastrophe occur — such as an automobile accident causing bodily injury for which you are found at fault — you could find yourself exposed to heavy financial burdens or even personal bankruptcy.

The Canadian Life and Health Insurance Compensation Corporation, usually known as CompCorp, is similar to PACICC. It is funded by member companies from the (L&H) insurance industry and provides protection should a member company become insolvent. CompCorp defines three classes of policies, each with different maximum protection. Class A includes all eligible policies that are not Class B or C policies, including life insurance policies. Class B policies are those that provide annuity and disability income, while Class C policies are those that provide health insurance. Let's review the protection provided for each class.

The maximum protection provided for a Class A life insurance policy is $200,000. An additional maximum of $60,000 of protection is separately available for each of four situations. These situations include variations of individual and group investment plans, such as RRSPs, whether or not they are registered under the Income Tax Act. The maximum protection provided for a Class B policy is $2,000 per month, and the maximum protection for a Class C policy is $60,000 in total payments per covered person.

The benefits and limitations associated with PACICC apply to CompCorp as well. On one hand, CompCorp insures against failure and provides swift payment. On the other hand, the payments are limited. It is clearly essential that you investigate the financial health of your potential insurance company. While some protection is provided should the company fail, the coverage is likely far less than that specified on your policy.

One way to overcome these limits is to diversify your insurance coverage across different companies, so that the coverage provided by each company is within the limits specified by PACICC and CompCorp. But the best protection is prevention — through choosing a policy from a financially healthy insurance company. Spending the time to investigate the financial health of potential insurance companies, as well as their level of customer service, is undoubtedly a tedious task, but taking the time will give you long-term peace of mind.

Choosing an Intermediary

We've discussed in detail the importance of the insurance company's reputation. But there is another player in the insurance game: the intermediary between the consumer and the insurance company. The behaviour and professionalism of the intermediary can strongly influence whether the correct insurance products are purchased.

You have four choices regarding the way you purchase insurance and with whom you deal:

1. *Agent* — An agent is a representative of a single insurance company who sells the products of that company exclusively, in return for the backup support that the company provides.
2. *Broker* — Brokers are not captive to a single insurance company, and therefore have greater flexibility in the policies they can offer. However, they also lack the support an insurance company provides to its agents.
3. *Direct seller* — This is a company that sells insurance over the telephone, typically at a discount, to customers who respond to advertising.
4. *Group plan* — Group plan insurance is a contract between an insurance company and an entity that represents a group, such as an employer or professional association. Individuals are covered by the plan through their connection with the group.

Why are consumers often apprehensive about purchasing insurance? Several characteristics of the purchase can lead to misgivings. First, insurance policies are extremely complex and difficult for consumers to understand. Therefore, consumers base their decisions on the advice of the intermediary, and can easily be manipulated. This is not a serious problem when you are purchasing insurance through a group plan, because group plans typically offer identical or similar insurance to all members of the group. Another benefit associated with group plans is that the group's purchasing power will likely result in a discounted price. On the other hand, the homogeneous nature of group policies may be restrictive, and the features associated with the policy may not be the most appropriate for all consumers.

Second, even after signing the contract, policyholders have no immediate way of evaluating the quality of the insurance policy. Such an evaluation can take place only when a claim is made, which may be years, even decades, in the future. Hence, the intermediary will not be held accountable over the short term.

Third, the intermediary selling the insurance has a dual role in representing the interests of both the consumer and the insurance company. Remember, even though the intermediary may officially represent either the consumer or the insurance company — for example, an agent is a representative of the insurance company — the intermediary also has a professional responsibility to the consumer. This dual role can lead to a conflict of interest in which the interests of the consumer conflict with the interests of the insurance company.

Fourth, the intermediary often visits the customer's residence to sell the insurance, and is therefore beyond supervision by the insurance company. The intermediary may behave in a manner inconsistent with the insurance company's ethics guidelines. This issue is clearly not associated with group plans, which are not sold in the consumer's home. It is also not an issue with direct selling, as telephone calls can be monitored.

A fifth characteristic, which is associated with agents and brokers, is that they work on commission. Consumers may suspect that the agent or broker is just after a quick buck, and that once they have signed on the dotted line, he or she will effectively disappear. One way to overcome these suspicions would be to avoid purchasing insurance from agents and brokers. However, rejecting their services might not be a good idea. A good agent or broker has expert knowledge about insurance that can help consumers avoid dangerous mistakes.

What can you do if you are worried that commissions motivate the advice you receive from the agent or broker, but you also require their expert knowledge? Consider paying an expert a flat fee to analyze your insurance portfolio and needs, and then use a cheaper method, such as a direct seller, to actually purchase the insurance. Another way to overcome suspicions — or to avoid a bad policy — is to do your research before the purchase. Find out about insurance (for example, by reading this book!). But, even after serious preparation, we must still rely on an insurance intermediary to help us make the right decision. The choice of intermediary is therefore crucial. Obtaining knowledge about insurance will enable you to ask the right questions when you are dealing with that intermediary.

Finally, common sense is also required. When choosing an agent or broker, you may wish to ask for references, or speak to friends and relatives for advice. Talking with someone who has first-hand experience with the agent or broker can give you insight as to whether or not he or she is right for you. You want someone with experience, and who will still be in the industry in 10 years. So you want to avoid an agent or broker at the beginning of his or her career, who may not be as knowledgeable as one with years of experience, and who may decide to change careers in a couple of years if things don't work out. You also want to avoid an agent close to retirement, who will be unavailable in the years ahead as your insurance needs change. For this reason, you might consider choosing an insurance agent close to your own age. As well, make sure you are comfortable about disclosing personal information to your agent or broker. For example, before choosing your sister-in-law as your insurance agent, ask yourself whether you really want her to know your medical history, driving record, or property value!

Are the misgivings that many of us feel when purchasing insurance warranted? Two studies performed in the United States provide some insight. The first study surveyed a mixture of insurance intermediaries that included agents, brokers ("independent agents"), direct sellers, and others.[26] The purpose of the study was to determine the extent to which they carried out — and believed others in their industry to carry out — unethical activities. The survey listed a number of unethical activities, including misrepresenting a competitor's product, twisting or replacing a policy without fully disclosing the consequences to the consumer, claiming that a policy is equivalent to a competitor's when in fact it is not, and offering lower premiums without disclosing the associated higher deductibles or other changes in classification.

The study found that insurance intermediaries are more likely to perceive that others in the industry engage in unethical activities than to engage (or admit to engaging) in such activities themselves. They also appear to understand clearly that these activities are, in fact, unethical. However, the researchers noted one disturbing, if not surprising, result: Top-producing intermediaries admit to participating in more unethical behaviour.

Another study tested the relationship between the degree to which life insurance agents depend on commissions for income

26 V. Howe, K. D. Hoffman, and D. W. Hardigree, "The Relationship Between Ethical and Customer-Oriented Service Provider Behaviors," *Journal of Business Ethics* 13 (1994), 497–506.

and their ethical behaviour.[27] The researchers asked whether the salesperson disclosed all of the available information to the client regardless of whether it was favourable or unfavourable to the client's interest. Interestingly, the study found no evidence that the type of compensation the agents received influenced their ethical behaviour. This result may be due to the sample used or to the tests performed. However, it does suggest that some of the suspicion about agents' and brokers' commissions may be misplaced.

Making a Claim

You've chosen your insurance provider and you've picked your policy. At this point you may be thinking that the rest is smooth sailing. All you need to do is sit back and pay your premiums every month. All the hard work has been done and all your difficult decisions have been made, and you won't have to think about insurance ever again. Unfortunately, your respite from thinking about insurance will last only until something happens and you have to make a claim.

What is the best way to go about making a claim? You might wonder why this is even an issue. Can't you just give the insurance provider a call and get the benefits you deserve? Unfortunately, this is often not the case — the claims process is not always as simple and straightforward as might be hoped.

Even before making a claim, you have to decide whether you should bother. If you can afford to avoid making the claim, you should do so. After all, the purpose of insurance is to provide protection for what you cannot pay for on your own, not to protect you against a $50 loss. Insurance companies are concerned about any household's tendency to engage in

27 N. B. Kurland, "Ethics, Incentives, and Conflicts of Interest: A Practical Solution," *Journal of Business Ethics* 14 (1995), 465–75.

behaviour that leads to claims. They consider a claim a bad signal, even if the actual compensation doesn't amount to much. While the insurance company is willing to reimburse you for small claims, they also take note of the number of claims you make. After too many claims, even if they are small in terms of the total dollar value of the benefits, the company may refuse to renew the insurance contract, leaving you vulnerable to a large financial burden should a serious event occur. One way to ensure that you don't engage in frivolous claim-making is to specify a high deductible wherever possible. This will affect your claim-making behaviour by removing the incentive to make small claims. As well, it will greatly reduce the cost of the insurance.

If you decide to go ahead with the claim, use common sense. The insurance company is not your friend, regardless of how warm and fuzzy their marketing campaign may be. They will provide you with the requested benefits only if you can demonstrate they are legally required to do so, according to the insurance contract you signed. So, before making a claim, read your policy. Is the loss covered? Is it clearly stated in the policy? Is it specifically excluded? Is it a grey area? Furthermore, make the claim quickly, and do temporary repairs at once; don't let the problem get worse. And don't wait until after your daughter's upcoming wedding, for example, to make that property claim, regardless of how busy you might be. The policy may specify a time period within which the claim must be made.

Insurance companies are large organizations, with detailed internal guidelines for dealing with claims. The more documentation you provide, the less likely it is that you will be asked questions that will slow down your claim or result in a rejection. Documentation might include police reports, repair estimates, damage inventories, letters from medical professionals, or receipts, as well as photos and videos of damage — anything that strengthens your claim.

But even with the best preparation, your claim may be turned down. Unfortunately, you may then have to take action. Recall the study that surveyed policyholders after Hurricane Hugo. That survey also measured the extent to which policyholders took action to get the desired settlement, such as hiring an attorney or contacting the media. The study found that of those who suffered the greatest amount of damage and had the highest level of uninsured losses, 52.6% threatened to take action, while only 40.8% actually did so.

So what can you do if a claim is turned down? You probably don't want to call your lawyer right away. Once you involve a lawyer, the insurance company and others associated with your claim will no longer deal with you directly. This will effectively take control of the situation out of your hands, and will exponentially increase the costs associated with making the claim.

Instead of calling your lawyer immediately, try working within the system. Speak to senior management in the insurance company and to the insurance company's ombudsperson, who deals with customer complaints. If that doesn't work, try going a step further — speak to the body that regulates insurance in your jurisdiction. Insurance is regulated at the provincial and territorial level, and also at the federal level through the Office of the Superintendent of Financial Institutions (OSFI). Complaints should generally be made initially at the provincial or territorial level, as the licensing and marketing of insurance companies is regulated at that level. OSFI, at the federal level, conducts reviews of insurance companies to determine their financial soundness.

Another useful resource to contact is an insurance industry association. The Insurance Bureau of Canada (IBC) deals with complaints associated with P&C insurance claims, and the Canadian Life and Health Insurance Association of Canada (CLHIA) handles complaints associated with L&H insurance claims. According to CLHIA, 900,000 people have contacted their Consumer Assistance Centre since 1973 with various enquiries, including complaints about their insurance companies.

One way to minimize the possibility of running into a roadblock when making insurance claims is to develop a relationship with both the insurance company and your intermediary. The insurance company is a lot more likely to be flexible when dealing with a long-term policyholder than it will be when dealing with a new one. And if you have a relationship with an agent or broker, he or she will be included as your advocate at claims time — a role that brokers and agents play where group plans and direct sellers do not. Often this advocacy more than makes up for the additional premiums you pay when using an agent or broker as an intermediary.

Summary Points

- Insurance companies work hard to develop a public image as reliable, traditional, and trustworthy. This is because an insurance policy is a long-term contract, based on trust. Policyholders pay premiums to insurance companies over a long period of time with the expectation (or hope) that the companies will provide the promised benefits when they make a claim in the future.
- Two dimensions that determine an insurance company's reputation are the degree to which it satisfies claims as promised, and the probability that it will fail before a claim is eventually made. Reputation can play a significant role in the insurance company's ability to set premiums. Therefore it is a serious mistake to choose a policy exclusively on the basis of premium size.

- The degree to which an insurance company satisfies claims as promised is a function of a number of factors. These include the company's flexibility when a claim is made, customer service provided, the ease with which the policyholder can contact a representative, the length of time until benefits are paid, and the company's renewability and cancellation policies, among other factors. Differences in the behaviour of insurance companies following an incident may appear minor when you are signing a contract, but they can have serious financial implications when it comes time to make a claim.
- Regardless of how flexible and oriented towards customer service an insurance provider may be, it will be unable to keep its promises if it is insolvent. The probability of the company failing before a claim is made is a function of factors such as the company's financial strength, operating performance, and market profile. Simply because an insurance company has a long history does not necessarily mean it won't fail, as the infamous Confederation Life collapse illustrates. Evidence suggests that industry ratings, which are based on a multitude of factors, are the best predictors of future failure.
- Organizations that are funded by member companies from the industry provide limited protection for policyholders of insurance companies that fail. The Property and Casualty Insurance Compensation Corporation (PACICC) provides protection if your P&C company fails, while the Canadian Life and Health Insurance Compensation Corporation (CompCorp) provides protection should your L&H insurance company fail. One way to overcome the limits of this protection is to diversify insurance coverage among different companies, so that the coverage provided by each company is no greater than the specified limits.

- Insurance can be purchased through agents, brokers, direct sellers, or group plans. A number of characteristics associated with insurance policies may lead to misgivings, and there are pros and cons associated with each method. If you are greatly concerned that commissions motivate the advice you receive from your intermediary, consider paying an expert a flat fee to analyze your insurance portfolio and needs, and then use a cheaper method to actually purchase the insurance. Another way to overcome suspicions — or to avoid a bad policy — is to obtain knowledge about the insurance industry beforehand.
- The claims process is often challenging. Even the decision to make a claim requires thought, because a claim sends a negative signal to the insurance company, regardless of the size of actual benefits. Should a claim be rejected, the policyholder should consider a number of avenues before using a lawyer, including pursuing the rejection with the insurance company, industry associations, and regulatory bodies.

How to Sound Intelligent

Some Questions to Ask When Purchasing Insurance

- Should I purchase insurance through an agent, broker, direct seller, or group plan?
- Is the agent or broker experienced, and will he or she still be in the industry in 10 years?
- Is the insurance company flexible when dealing with a claim?
- What kind of customer service does the insurance company provide?
- Do my friends and relatives have any experiences to relate regarding the insurance company or intermediary?
- What are the insurance company's renewability and cancellation policies?

- What is the financial health of the insurance company? How is it rated?
- Have I considered diversifying my insurance coverage among different companies, so that the coverage provided by each is no greater than the limits specified by PACICC and CompCorp?

Some Questions to Ask When Making a Claim

- Do I really want to make the claim, considering how it will affect my claims history?
- Have I carefully read my policy to determine whether I am covered?
- Am I making the claim without delay?
- Have I carefully documented the claim?

Some Questions to Ask When a Claim Is Rejected

- Have I tried contacting the insurance company's ombudsperson?
- Have I tried to contact consumer assistance representatives at the IBC and CLHIA?
- Have I tried contacting the body that regulates insurance in my jurisdiction?
- Am I aware of the implications, in terms of control over the claim and costs, associated with using a lawyer to represent me?

8

Insurance Fraud

What could be more humanitarian than helping alcoholics and drug addicts? Two brothers offered 40 homeless alcoholics and drug addicts jobs and a place to live. They were also thoughtful enough to take out a hundred life insurance policies on these unfortunate people, using forged health records and naming fake beneficiaries. Their hospitality didn't end there. They provided free alcohol and drugs at their "homeless shelter" — hoping to accelerate the demise of their residents and collect on their insurance policies. Sadly, seven of their "guests" did die. That wasn't enough for the brothers, so they hired hit men to kill some others. Fortunately they were caught before any more died, and were eventually sent to jail.[28]

The above true story suggests that crime doesn't pay. Or does it? The Canadian Coalition Against Insurance Fraud (CCAIF), an organization founded by insurance companies, estimates that approximately $1.3 billion is paid out per year for fraudulent insurance claims. Unfortunately it seems that crime

28 Story from the U.S.-based Coalition Against Insurance Fraud.

does pay — and it's the insurance companies doing the paying. And when insurance companies pay, policyholders do, too — with higher premiums.

Our objective in this chapter is not to try to talk you out of participating in insurance fraud. If the eighth commandment ("thou shalt not steal") plus modern mores, sheer embarrassment, and fear of a jail term can't do the job, how could two professors possibly frighten you out of committing a crime? The purpose of this chapter is to describe the extent of insurance fraud in Canada, how it hurts society, and what society (and the insurance industry) is doing to fight back. We also illustrate insurance scams by considering some schemes that the bad guys — the con artists, hustlers, and cheats — use to try to separate you from your money.

What Is Insurance Fraud?

Insurance is society's security net. It compensates millions of people for their stolen possessions, accidents, changes in health, or death. However, many people try to take advantage of the insurance system to obtain benefits without a legitimate claim. This devious behaviour is called insurance fraud.

Insurance fraud is defined by CCAIF as "any act or omission with a view to illegally obtain an insurance benefit." Fraudulent acts include fabricated claims, inflated or padded legitimate claims, false statements on insurance applications, besides others. Any dishonest or opportunistic behaviour used to obtain insurance benefits is considered a crime, according to section 380(1) of the Canadian Criminal Code. Hence, insurance fraud is a crime.

Insurance fraud can take two forms. First, the fraudster — that's the person committing the fraud — may attempt to make an insurance company pay compensation for an event that never happened. For example, an individual may fake a car accident in hopes of collecting from his insurance company. Consider the following true story.[29]

A man claimed that he had been injured in a car accident. His story sounded somewhat suspicious and the insurance company decided to put him under video surveillance. But the surveillance picked up more than they bargained for. Not only did the videotape show a perfectly healthy man going about his daily routine, it also demonstrated that part of his daily routine was car theft! Moral of the story: It takes a criminal to do the crime.

A fraudster may also exaggerate an otherwise genuine claim with the hope of getting more cash than he rightfully deserves. For example, a person may claim that her car stereo system, stolen during a robbery, was worth $1,000, when in fact she bought it for $25. Or consider the following true story.[30]

A man was in the passenger seat of a car that was involved in a crash. After making a claim for injuries, he received over $100,000 in benefits from the insurance company as compensation. Unfortunately for the man, his neighbours anonymously called the insurance company to let them know that in spite of his "injuries," the man was able to renovate his house, work in the garden, and jump around on a trampoline. It seems that he had really "bounced back" from his exaggerated injuries!

Most Canadians are unlikely to engage in the first type of fraud, as that kind of elaborate scheme is typically reserved for the criminal mind. But the second type of fraud poses a moral dilemma for some people. After all, you might argue in a weak moment, you've been paying such high insurance premiums for *so* long. And it would be so *unfair* if you didn't get some of that money back. And so little effort is required as well — it's *only* a little white lie. And the insurance company has *so* much money, etc., etc. Unfortunately, this slippery moral slope has led many

29 Story from the Canadian Coalition Against Insurance Fraud.
30 Ibid.

people — who would normally be aghast at being accused of criminal activity — to violate the Criminal Code and risk a criminal record, fines, and possibly jail time.

The evidence suggests that many have morally slipped, for insurance fraud is a leading source of criminal profits in North America. A 1996 study commissioned by CCAIF examined approximately 500 paid and closed claims files to determine the extent to which the claims were fraudulent. Of the 500 closed claims, a full 6.5% contained obvious fraud, but the claims had been paid without being checked by the company investigator or the Insurance Crime Prevention Bureau (now known as the Investigative Services Division). In addition, the examination discovered that another 6% of the 500 claims indicated potential fraud. Based on this study, CCAIF estimates that approximately 10% to 15% of every dollar of your insurance premium is spent on paying for insurance fraud.

Other evidence of the extent of fraudulent claims comes from analysis of claims in the United States. A statistical study of automobile bodily injury insurance claims found that 10% appear to be fraudulent, while build-up — inflation of damages associated with an otherwise valid claim — was between 35% and 48%.[31] Another study found that build-up is especially prevalent with injuries that are difficult to diagnose objectively, such as lower back pain or spinal problems.[32] This study suggests the obvious, that people are more likely to exaggerate a claim if they think they can get away with it.

It's not only policyholders who perpetrate insurance fraud. Even some insurance agents have been caught! In 1991, detectives in Toronto uncovered a scam organized by life insurance

31 H. I. Weisberg and R. A. Derrig, "Fraud and Automobile Insurance: A Report on the Baseline Study of Bodily Injury Claims in Massachusetts," *Journal of Insurance Regulation* 9 (1991), 427–541.
32 G. Dionne and P. St-Michel, "Workers' Compensation and Moral Hazard," *Review of Economics and Statistics* 73 (1991), 236–44.

agents. It seems that some life insurance companies were paying to their agents commissions equivalent to 1.5 times the first year's premiums. So some agents began taking out phony policies and paying for them out of their own pockets in order to get their hands on the commissions. Then, after the first year, they cancelled the policies.[33]

Who Gets Hurt by Insurance Fraud?

Let's be honest — many people are resentful towards their insurance companies. The common perception is that insurance companies are charging high premiums for little received in return. Whether that's an accurate perception or not, it doesn't endear the insurance industry to many. Some people have had bad experiences with insurance companies. Perhaps they had a policy or claim rejected, or they may have received the bureaucratic runaround when trying to clarify issues related to their policies.

It is, therefore, rather remarkable that public opinion polls conducted for the Insurance Bureau of Canada show that most Canadians are solidly against insurance fraud, even though many practise it. A poll conducted in 1997 suggests that only 4% of Canadians consider insurance fraud acceptable. A 1995 poll suggests that only 5% believe padding a claim is acceptable, although 50% believe that claims exaggeration is common, according to a 1996 poll. Another poll conducted in 1996 suggests that 57% of Canadians would be willing to undergo more thorough investigation of claims. And a poll conducted in 1995 suggests that 76% of Canadians believe that the responsibility for stopping fraud is shared between the insurance companies and their customers.

33 *Financial Post* 90:19 (May 11/13, 1996), IBN2.

These poll results are quite surprising, as they suggest mass support for insurance companies in their fight against fraud. How can we explain this widespread support? Part of the answer lies in an information campaign by the insurance industry through CCAIF. Since its founding in 1994, CCAIF has engaged in research, public opinion polling, and newsletter publication and has formed an alliance with Crime Stoppers, among other activities. The information campaign has been effective. While polls conducted in 1994 suggested that 20% of Canadians found insurance fraud acceptable, only 4% believed so in 1997.

However, the information campaign provides only a partial explanation. The deeper reason for public support of the fight against fraud is the realization that, ultimately, the public pays for insurance fraud. Insurance fraud is not only a crime against the insurance company. While we risk sounding too dramatic, the facts suggest that insurance fraud hurts society at many levels.

Insurance fraud leads to honest policyholders paying increased premiums, because insurance companies must raise their premiums to cover their fraud-related losses. The decision by a few policyholders to claim cash fraudulently thus indirectly places a financial burden on all policyholders. A CCAIF study mentioned earlier suggested that 10% to 15% of every dollar you pay for your insurance premium goes towards paying for insurance fraud. If that fraud premium figure is accurate, insurance fraud may play a more important role in determining the total premium than any other factor, such as gender or claims experience. That makes sense; after all, any cash paid out to satisfy insurance claims comes from the pool of money obtained from premium payments. The more cash that goes out, the more cash must go in.

To get a better picture of the impact of insurance fraud, let's compare it to a more traditional source of claims, a natural disaster — specifically, the 1998 Quebec ice storm. According to the Insurance Bureau of Canada, damage from the ice storm resulted in 700,000 claims totalling $1.44 billion. This amount placed a serious burden on insurance companies. Yet the same companies and their policyholders pay out an estimated $1.3 billion *every year* because of insurance fraud.

And it's not only insurance companies and their policyholders who lose. Insurance fraud is costly to those who are not policyholders as well. When someone sets a fire in hopes of defrauding the insurance company, firefighters risk their lives and expend valuable resources trying to stop the fire. When someone makes a fraudulent accident claim, police resources that would be better used for other purposes are wasted on investigating the "accident." A health care professional may spend valuable time with a patient who is faking an injury — who truly doesn't need the services — while others wait in line. In addition to the $1.3 billion that insurance companies pay out for fraudulent claims, an additional $1 billion a year of society's resources, according to CCAIF's estimates, is wasted by insurance fraud. The wasted money and resources are bad enough, but another horrific consequence of insurance fraud is the injury and death of innocent people who die from insurance fraud gone wrong, such as arson or staged accidents.

How Does the Insurance Industry Prevent Insurance Fraud?

Three interrelated methods are commonly used to prevent insurance fraud. The first method is educating the public. As we have discussed, the insurance industry has developed an effective information program through CCAIF, which explains to the public the costs and risks associated with insurance fraud.

The second method is setting penalties for fraud. Fraud is a criminal act that can result in criminal charges, civil suits, and denial of claims. Let's consider a specific example of penalties for fraud. The Insurance Corporation of British Columbia (ICBC) is British Columbia's provincially mandated automobile insurance provider (as mentioned in Chapter 5, B.C.'s automobile insurance is administered by the government). ICBC specifies three types of penalties that people who attempt to defraud it may face:

1. *Criminal charges* — Because of recent legislation, it's a specific criminal offence to attempt to obtain money or other benefits from ICBC by providing false or misleading information. Anyone convicted of a fraud-related criminal offence faces up to two years in jail, up to $25,000 in fines for a first conviction, and up to $50,000 in fines for subsequent convictions.
2. *Civil suits* — ICBC claims it has a policy of suing those caught making fraudulent claims, with the intention of recovering both the funds and punitive damages, as well as fees for investigation, claims handling, and hiring experts.
3. *Denial of claim* — If an individual makes a wilfully false statement to claim more than he or she is entitled to, legislation permits ICBC to deny the *entire* claim.

The third of the three interrelated methods of preventing insurance fraud is monitoring — investigating and identifying fraudulent claims. Public education may convince some people not to participate in insurance fraud, while fear of penalties may motivate others not to bother. However, a penalty will motivate behaviour only if there is a reasonable likelihood that people engaged in insurance fraud will actually be caught. To improve the probability of catching them, firms must actively investigate and identify fraudulent claims. The resulting penalties are typically a function of the insurer's willingness to pursue fraud. For example, Ontario's Workplace Safety and Insurance Board (WSIB) announced a "zero tolerance for fraud" policy in May 1997. In 1998, the Special Investigations Branch of the board laid no fewer than 429 charges, of which 78 were under the Criminal Code of Canada and the remainder under the Provincial Offences Act. According to the WSIB's figures, this resulted in a total savings of $14.9 million, of which $4.4 million came about through discovery of parallel fraud in the welfare system.

However, and quite remarkably, firms are often reluctant to pursue investigations on their own. Why the reluctance? First, insurance companies want to close claim files as quickly as possible, and are therefore reluctant to engage in lengthy investigations. Second, investigations are often costly. To investigate a claim fully, a firm could spend thousands of dollars in fees for experts such as professional locksmiths and arson investigators. Third, the court system is often backlogged — hence, time-consuming — and demanding about the type of evidence it will accept. Therefore, pursuing fraudsters in the civil and criminal courts wastes valuable resources.

To overcome these obstacles, insurance companies have pursued strategies to make investigation of insurance fraud more efficient. One such strategy is to form industry coalitions to investigate and keep track of fraud. In Canada, the P&C insurance industry has formed such a coalition, the Investigative Services Division (ISD) of the Insurance Bureau of Canada. The ISD — formerly the Insurance Crime Prevention Bureau (ICPB) — maintains loss-information databases and conducts investigations at the request of member companies. Members, in turn, provide claims information that includes the name and address of the claimant, the claimant's date of birth, the date of the loss that led to the claim, the name of the insurer, and the amount paid out. This information is added to the ISD's database, which effectively keeps track of most P&C claims made in Canada.

As well, the ISD will investigate a suspicious fire, automobile theft, or other property loss if requested to do so by a member. That an investigation is taking place may be disclosed to the individual under investigation, should that individual make such a request. However, the person being investigated can obtain the actual content of the investigation only from the insurance company that requested the investigation. The ISD also engages in related activities such as supplying polygraph tests and providing vehicles with new VINs (vehicle identification numbers), and has formed partnerships with organizations such as the Canadian Police Information Centre, Interpol, and the Canadian Association of Fire Investigators, among others.

As an example of an investigation in which the ISD played a role, consider "Project Slip," an investigation that resulted in more than 30 arrests in the Greater Toronto area in July 2000.[34] At the time, the Toronto Transit Commission (TTC) had a no-fault payout policy. The policy mandated that the TTC pay out claims against it within 14 days, placing severe restrictions on the transit authority's ability to investigate claims for possible fraud. Taking advantage of this policy, a group of fraudsters — allegedly including doctors, chiropractors, and a paralegal — recruited people to either fake injuries on TTC property or file false accident claims. The cunning fraudsters had their recruits claim injuries that can't be identified objectively (such as soft-tissue damage), but which are designated as injuries through highly subjective diagnosis. The estimated total cost of the

34 Factual information from V. Spencer, "Cracking the Case: Investigating Insurance Fraud," *Canadian Underwriter* (November 2000).

scam to the insurance industry and the Ontario Health Insurance Plan (OHIP) was in the millions. Unfortunately for the fraudsters, phone tips led to an investigation in which the ISD (then known as the ICPB) assisted police in tracking down claims through its databases.

Other companies, such as Corporate Investigation Services and Quality Investigative Services, also specialize in providing services such as background investigations, surveillance, and claims profiles. Insurance companies may choose to use the services of one of these companies during an investigation.

Insurance companies also use technology to make investigation of insurance fraud more cost-efficient. Investigative systems are used to analyze databases for potential fraud. At its most basic level, the objective of an investigative system is to detect similarities in claims that might be an indication of fraud. For example, the system may analyze whether one person has made similar claims over a given period of time. Or it may raise a red flag, suggesting caution, when a specific characteristic is associated with a claim, such as lack of witnesses to an accident. If enough red flags are raised, the company will investigate further.

Consider a slightly more complicated example. An insurance company wants to investigate whether any of the dental insurance claims submitted by 5,000 dentists for a given procedure are fraudulent. The company uses an investigative system to compare the claims of each dentist for the given procedure with the average claim of all 5,000 dentists. The insurance firm may find that the claims submitted by 25 dentists are well above average, and therefore warrant further investigation. Following this investigation, 23 of the dentists may be found to be legitimate, while 2 are not. While avoiding investigating all 5,000 dentists — a costly endeavour — technology makes possible the identification of fraudulent dentists among them.

In all of these examples, a smart fraudster could of course easily avoid detection. John Doe may be J. Doe in one jurisdiction and John L. Doe in another. Organized fraudsters will make sure they have "witnesses" willing to come forward to attest to an event. As well, a clever fraudster takes pains to submit claims that are neither unusually large nor unusually small. To detect fraud in these situations, the investigative system must be capable of identifying more subtle patterns in the data. To enable this, the system may incorporate more databases, use more sophisticated database technologies, and use more complex statistical methodologies when searching for patterns. For example, artificial neural networks are now included in some investigative systems. These complex systems of computation methodology are loosely modelled on the structure of the brain, and are used in investment analysis, signature analysis, and sophisticated weaponry, among other applications.

Regardless of the technology used, investigative systems require human input to decide exactly which values of which information variables constitute red flags. Evidence suggests that the choice of red flags is quite subjective. In an interesting study, researchers gave a single set of claims to two adjusters, requesting an independent analysis from each.[35] Each of them classified 9% of the claims as fraudulent — but only 1.8% of the claims were classified as fraudulent by both adjusters. Clearly, there can be widespread discrepancy among experts regarding what exactly constitutes a red flag. Researchers use statistical techniques to identify which indicators are the best red flags, but there are constraints on the number of questions that can be asked of a system, as well as limitations on computing power.

35 H. I. Weisberg and R. A. Derrig, *Quantitative Methods for Detecting Fraudulent Automobile Bodily Injury Claims* (Boston: Automobile Insurers Bureau of Massachusetts, 1993). Fraudulent Claims Payment Filing. D.O.I. Docket G93-24, 1994.

Insurance Scams

So far, we've considered insurance fraud in which policyholders engage in fraudulent acts with a view to illegally obtaining insurance benefits. However, quite often the policyholder is the *victim* of a fraudulent insurance scam. While most Canadian insurance companies (and other participants in the industry) are legitimate, there are always individuals, organized fraud schemes, and companies that will try to deceive you in numerous ways. The following are a few examples of companies that have perpetrated insurance scams.

A Brampton, Ontario, man swindled thousands of dollars from car owners and drivers in Greater Toronto by selling false auto insurance certificates. The man was operating an insurance provider — aptly named the Affordable Insurance Group — without a license, and even had the chutzpah to advertise his phony product! After an investigation, the Financial Services Commission of Ontario (FSCO) issued a cease-and-desist order, seized the Affordable Insurance Group's books and other property, and contacted customers to inform them that they had no insurance coverage. In October 1999, the swindler pleaded guilty in court to carrying out business and advertising as an insurance agent without a license. He was ordered to pay a $10,000 fine as well as restitution payments to the victims of his scam.

The Affordable Insurance Group was not the only fraudulent insurance provider operating in the Greater Toronto area. Here's another example. In July 2000, FSCO issued a cease-and-desist order against two companies, Crump Barter Services and Executive Barter. The companies were advertising a bogus insurance product for an outfit named Tri-Continental Exchange Ltd., which was also slapped with a cease-and-desist order. In May 2001, the operator of Tri-Continental Exchange was fined $75,000 for ignoring the cease-and-desist order to stop selling phony insurance. The superintendent of FSCO at the time, Dina Palozzi, didn't pull any punches in the following statement: "Anyone owning or driving a car who has dealt with Tri-Continental Exchange . . . or anyone else like them, is in violation of the Compulsory Automobile Insurance Act. By buying into this scam, these owners and drivers do not have valid automobile insurance in Ontario."[36]

Avoiding illegitimate insurance providers is of paramount importance. People who purchase invalid policies may be allowed only minimal medical and rehabilitation benefits if they are in an accident. They also might not be able to claim wage-loss benefits and could even lose their right to sue. In addition, they could be personally responsible for civil actions. Unfortunately, people tend to be much too trusting! To use a metaphor, if you buy a boat with holes in it, don't be surprised if it sinks the first time out on the lake. Similarly, if you buy insurance from an unlicensed broker or agent, don't be surprised if you face bankruptcy and personal financial ruin after your first accident. As you can see, making sure your insurance provider is licensed is an obvious, yet essential, first step when deciding to buy insurance.

Besides those willing to sell you a phony policy, there are also con artists who are more than willing to recruit you into their latest scam, for example, a "medical mill." The ISD defines a medical mill as a group of health care professionals who use fraudulent billing practices to rip off patients and insurance companies. For example, a doctor may recommend unnecessary surgery for a soft-tissue injury that is difficult to diagnose. Unscrupulous providers of legal services may funnel people to a medical mill in return for a kickback.

36 "Phony Insurer Hit with $75,000 Fine," press release from the Financial Services Commission of Ontario, *Canada NewsWire* (May 18, 2001).

There are individuals and companies out there who are plainly ready to bilk us. What can consumers do on their own to avoid being victims of insurance fraud? Let's consider the different types of scams you could fall into: personal injury scams and medical tricks, car cons, and insurance purchasing rip-offs.

Medical Scams

Possibly the last thing on your mind following an accident is whether you can trust your legal advisor or health care professional. Unfortunately, unscrupulous individuals are fully aware that you have other concerns. They may try to involve you in an insurance scam that could result in your going through unnecessary medical procedures. Or their activities could result in the police and your insurance company suspecting that you are a perpetrator of insurance fraud — a pseudo-patient with fake or exaggerated injuries who has been recruited by the medical mill. The ISD provides a number of tips to make sure you don't fall into this trap. Watch out for the following red flags:

- unsolicited lawyers who contact you immediately following an accident
- a lawyer who advises you to see a specific doctor (the ISD claims that this type of behaviour is a good indicator of a medical mill)
- doctors prescribing excessive treatment (seek a second opinion)

If you suspect that you are receiving "treatment" from a medical mill, make sure that you inform your claim representative and the ISD. If you are correct, your involvement is much more likely to be perceived as innocent if you raise the alarm first.

Automobile Accident Scams

When we are driving, we keep a sharp lookout for a number of dangers — other drivers, bad road conditions, poor visibility, and the occasional flying truck tire. The last thing on our minds is the possibility that one of our fellow drivers will slam his or her car into us *on purpose*. Yet this does happen — and it's not entirely irrational. Consider an insurance fraudster who is looking to win big in the liability lottery. She may already know the injury she is going to claim — likely a soft-tissue injury, or maybe a pre-existing condition, such as a broken shoulder. All she needs now is an accident. And the fancier your car, the fraudster will assume, the more third party liability insurance you are likely to hold.

Yes, such people do exist. And while we don't suggest you become paranoid — surely most of your fellow drivers are, like yourself, perfect angels — but in certain situations you may want to keep an eye out for fraudsters. For example, be careful when turning into a lane from which two automobiles, one driven by you and the other by the fraudster, can turn left simultaneously. Automobiles turning left into centre lanes are targets for sideswiping by fraudsters. And if you do get into an accident, count the number of passengers in the other car and get their names and contact information. "Passengers" — and their lawyers — have a strange habit of emerging after accidents. It also wouldn't hurt to carry a camera in the car — just to make sure the owner of the other automobile doesn't take a sledgehammer to his vehicle later to increase his claim.

Phony Insurance Scams

While most of us don't expect a fellow driver to purposely involve us in an accident, we are suspicious when purchasing insurance. Unfortunately, our suspicion is normally focused on price and face value — how much are the premiums, and what do we get in return? We hardly ever consider the possibility of being scammed. In our efforts to keep premiums low, we tend not to consider the possibility that the policy isn't worth the piece of paper it's written on. As with the FSCO cease-and-desist orders we discussed earlier, there are many people out there more than willing to give you a good price on an insurance policy — a phony insurance policy. This tends to occur more frequently with automobile insurance than with other insurance products. This may be because the con artist is betting on the driver's not getting into a serious accident. Further, because automobile insurance is mandatory, many naive individuals think of the insurance certificate as just another piece of paper they need to keep in their wallet in order to be allowed to drive, like a driver's license, and nothing more. So if they are offered the "piece of paper" at a discount, they will buy it, no questions asked. As we mentioned earlier, this is a terrible mistake — without insurance, or with phony insurance, drivers leave themselves vulnerable.

One must use common sense to avoid being sold phony insurance. Check whether the insurance company is properly licensed. Be very careful about purchasing insurance from a door-to-door salesperson, over the phone, or on the Internet. Never sign anything before reading the fine print. Don't purchase the first policy you find.

Be suspicious. Keep your senses on maximum alert for red flags. Is the agent or broker being evasive? Do you have to pay in cash? Are you given a copy of the policy? Finally, don't be greedy — ask yourself, do the premiums make sense for the product I am purchasing? If the price for the insurance is half the price quoted by others, that should raise suspicions. You might be getting a good deal, but, as the saying goes, there is no such thing as a free lunch. If the deal sounds too good to be true, it's probably not true!

Summary Points

- Insurance fraud can take two forms. The fraudster may attempt to make the insurance company pay compensation for events that never happened or may exaggerate an otherwise genuine claim. Most Canadians are unlikely to engage in the first type of fraud, but may face a moral dilemma regarding the second. Evidence suggests that insurance fraud is widespread in Canada.
- The insurance industry has engaged in effective public information campaigns to support its fight against insurance fraud. However, the widespread support it enjoys is due to public realization that, ultimately, the public pays for insurance fraud. Policyholders face higher insurance premiums because of fraud, and society wastes valuable human and financial resources.
- The fight against insurance fraud is threefold. First, the industry engages in public education. Second, fraudsters face penalties such as criminal charges, civil suits, and denial of claims. Third, the industry engages in monitoring — the identification and investigation of fraudulent claims.
- Insurance firms are often reluctant to pursue investigations on their own because of their desire to close claim files quickly, high costs associated with investigations, and a demanding justice system. To overcome these obstacles, insurance companies form coalitions to investigate fraud, and use investigative systems to analyze databases for potential fraud.
- While most participants in the insurance industry are legitimate, there are individuals and organizations engaged in insurance scams. These may include unlicensed insurance companies selling phony insurance policies, medical mills, and those wishing to stage an accident. To avoid becoming a victim, people must be cautious when purchasing insurance,

at an accident scene, and when dealing with legal and health professionals.

How to Sound Intelligent

Some Questions to Ask When Purchasing Insurance

- What is the reputation of the broker or agent?
- Does the insurance company have a license to sell insurance?
- Are the premiums too low for the type of insurance I am buying? If so, why?
- What does the fine print say?
- Is the insurance agent being evasive?

Some Questions to Ask Following an Insurable Event

- In an accident, have I carefully documented the number and names of passengers in the other vehicle, as well as the amount of damage to the other car?
- Do I trust my legal representative?
- Is my legal representative suggesting I see a specific doctor?
- Are the health care professionals prescribing excessive treatment?
- Have I carefully documented all dealings with my legal representative and health care professionals?

Conclusion

September 11, 2001

We have been staring at the TV in complete disbelief for the past 12 hours. Our plans were to spend the day writing a concluding chapter on the importance of life insurance, health insurance, and property insurance. But all we can think about are the thousands of people trapped under the rubble and the possibly tens of thousands of widows and orphans that have been created by this horrendous tragedy.

Luckily, our family and loved ones were out of harm's way and have all been accounted for. But the same cannot be said for some of our business acquaintances, colleagues, and associates who worked at the ominously named Ground Zero.

At a time like this, money, wealth, or fortune is the last thing on people's minds. But, as time goes on, and the extended families of the victims start down the path to healing, financial issues will take centre stage. Mortgages have to be paid, tuition has to be covered, and children must be cared for.

We have no idea to what extent the people affected by this tragedy can alleviate some of their pain by knowing they do not have to worry about financial matters. But if there has ever been a reminder that human life is a fragile blessing that cannot be taken for granted, it was the events of September 11.

We therefore take this final opportunity to remind you that your human capital is just as valuable as your financial capital. No amount of money will be able to replace the love and care you give to your family. But, at the very least, you might derive some measure of comfort from knowing that they will be looked after financially.

Please take care of yourself and stay safe.

Information Resources

Insurance Information

A. M. Best Canada Ltd.
This organization provides ratings of insurance companies and detailed information about how it determines those ratings.
Web site: www.ambest.ca
E-mail: canada.webmaster@ambest.com
Telephone: (416) 363-8266
Address: 133 Richmond Street West, Suite 600
Toronto, ON M5H 2L3

Canadian Association of Insurance and Financial Advisors
This professional association, which represents insurance and financial advisors across Canada, provides information about both financial advisors and insurance products.
Web site: www.caifa.com
E-mail: info@caifa.com
Telephone: 1-800-563-5822
Address: 350 Bloor Street East, 2nd Floor
Toronto, ON M4W 3W8

Canadian Coalition Against Insurance Fraud

The coalition was founded by Canadian insurers to help curb property and casualty (P&C) insurance fraud. Its services include information about insurance fraud and "top ten" lists of insurance fraud cases.

Web site: www.fraudcoalition.org
E-mail: webmaster@fraudcoalition.org
Telephone: (416) 362-4550
Address: 151 Yonge Street, 18th floor
Toronto, ON M5C 2W7

Canadian Life and Health Insurance Association

The CLHIA is the national trade association of non-government life and health (L&H) insurers. It provides detailed information about the L&H industry, as well as informative publications and consumer assistance.

Web site: www.clhia.ca
E-mail: info@clhia.ca
Telephone: 1-800-268-8099 (English)
1-800-361-8070 (French)
Address: 1 Queen Street East, Suite 1700
Toronto, ON M5C 2X9

Canadian Life and Health Insurance Compensation Corporation (CompCorp)

CompCorp was created by the life and health (L&H) insurance industry in Canada to provide Canadian policyholders with limited protection in the event of insolvency of their life or health insurance company.

Web site: www.compcorp.ca
E-mail: info@compcorp.ca
Telephone: 1-800-268-8099
Address: 1 Queen Street East, Suite 1600
Toronto, ON M5C 2X9

Insurance Brokers Association of Canada

The IBAC is the national trade organization of independent property and casualty (P&C) insurance brokers in Canada. It provides con-

sumer information about the benefits of using insurance brokers, and is a useful source of information on surviving natural disasters.
Web site: www.ibac.ca
E-mail: info@ibac.ca
Telephone: (416) 367-1831
Address: 155 University Avenue, Suite 1920
Toronto, ON M5H 3B7

Insurance Bureau of Canada
The IBC is the national trade association of non-government property and casualty (P&C) insurers. It provides detailed information about the P&C industry, as well as about home and automobile insurance products.
Web site: www.ibc.ca
E-mail: webmaster@ibc.ca
Telephone: British Columbia: 1-877-772-3777; Prairie provinces, Northwest Territories, and Nunavut: 1-800-377-6378; Ontario: 1-800-387-2880; Quebec: 1-800-361-5131; Atlantic provinces: 1-800-565-7189
Address: 151 Yonge Street, Suite 1800
Toronto, ON M5C 2W7

Property and Casualty Insurance Compensation Corporation
This organization was created by the property and casualty (P&C) insurance industry in Canada to provide Canadian policyholders with limited protection in the event of insolvency of their property or casualty insurance company.
Web site: www.pacicc.ca
E-mail: info@pacicc.com
Telephone: 1-888-564-9199
Address: 20 Richmond Street East, Suite 210
Toronto, ON M5C 2R9

Vehicle Information Centre of Canada
This division of the Insurance Bureau of Canada was founded by Canada's automobile insurance industry to analyze the costs associated with insuring different models of cars. It provides detailed information

on car theft, road safety, and vehicle insurance. In addition, it can provide information about the Canadian Loss Experience Automobile Rating system (CLEAR).
Web site: www.vicc.com
E-mail: vicc@vicc.com
Telephone: (416) 445-1883
Address: 240 Duncan Mill Road, Suite 700
Toronto, ON M3B 1Z4

Regulators

Office of the Superintendent of Financial Institutions
The OSFI is the primary regulator of federally chartered financial institutions and federally administered pension plans. Its mission is to safeguard policyholders, depositors, and pension plan members from undue loss.
Web site: www.osfi-bsif.gc.ca
E-mail: extcomm@osfi-bsif.gc.ca
Telephone: 1-800-385-8647
Address: 255 Albert Street
Ottawa, ON K1A 0H2

Other Regulators
Information and links to territorial and provincial regulators are available through the OSFI Web site at:
www.osfi-bsif.gc.ca/eng/links.asp?ref=links.

Journals

Journal of Risk and Insurance
This periodical is a publication of the American Risk and Insurance Association.
Web site: www.aria.org/jri
E-mail: aria@cpcuiia.org
Telephone: (610) 640-1997

Address: 716 Providence Road
P.O. Box 3028
Malvern, PA 19355-0728 U.S.A.

North American Actuarial Journal
This is a publication of the Society of Actuaries in the United States.
Web site: www.soa.org/bookstore/naaj.html
E-mail: bhaynes@soa.org
Telephone: (847) 706-3526
Address: Society of Actuaries
P.O. Box 95668
Chicago, IL 60694 U.S.A

Sources and Further Reading

Chapter 1: Life Insurance and the Theory of Insurance

For more information about life insurance and how it relates to the larger issue of financial planning, please see *Personal Financial Planning* by K. Ho and C. Robinson, 3rd edition (Toronto: Captus Press, 2000). The mortality probabilities are from Statistics Canada.

Chapter 2: Longevity Insurance

This chapter draws heavily from a research report written for the Florida State Board of Administration entitled "The Ideal Retirement Annuity." Material is also quoted from "Mortality Swaps and Tax Arbitrage in the Canadian Insurance Market," by M. A. Milevsky and N. Charupat, in *Journal of Risk and Insurance* 68:2 (June 2001) and from "Optimal Annuitization Policies: Analysis of the Options," by M. A. Milevsky, in *North American Actuarial Journal* 5:1 (January 2001). All data are from CANNEX Financial Exchanges (Toronto).

The probability calculations for Table 2.1 were performed as follows. There are, of course, four possibilities: (1) both are dead by age 85, (2) both are alive at age 85, (3) the husband is alive and the wife is dead by age 85, and (4) the wife is alive and the husband is dead by age 85. Mathematically, the probabilities of these four events must add up to 100%. In other words, (Probability of Event 1) + (Probability of Event 2) + (Probability of Event 3) + (Probability of Event 4) = 100%.

In the text, we state that for married couples, at least one of them will still be alive at 85 in over 70% of the cases. To calculate the chances that at least one of them will live to 85, we simply have to subtract from 100% the probability that both will die by age 85 (Event 1). Then we will be left with the sum of the probabilities (P) of the three events we are interested in: (2) both husband and wife are alive, (3) the husband is alive and the wife is dead, and (4) the wife is alive and the husband is dead.

This means that 100% – (P Event 1) = (P Event 2) + (P Event 3) + (P Event 4). The odds that neither of them survive (P Event 1) are calculated by multiplying the odds of the wife not surviving to 85 by the odds of the husband not surviving. Therefore, 72.2% is the probability that at least one will survive to age 85. Contrast that with the wife's and husband's individual chances of living to age 85 (52% and 41%, respectively). The idea is that there is a high certainty that at least one will get to that age.

Of course, we should mention that some actuaries and demographers have documented a "broken heart" effect, which tends to increase the odds — just slightly — of one spouse dying just after the other has passed away. So, to be very precise, we should say that the above calculation assumes complete independence between the two events.

Chapter 3: Health Insurance and Travel Insurance

This chapter relies heavily on information from the Canada Health Act Annual Report produced by Health Canada for 1999–2000. We also use information from the Canadian Life and Health Insurance Association, *Maclean's* magazine, the Canadian Institute for Health Information, an Ipsos-Reid poll conducted for the Canadian Medical Association, the *Journal of the American Medical Association*, *Health Affairs*, the Conference Board of Canada, and an EKOS Research Associates poll quoted in *Maclean's*. The Blue Cross quotes are from their online quoting system. Information from a number of other Canadian insurance providers is also used.

Chapter 4: Disability Insurance and Critical Illness Insurance

We use statistical information from the 1991 Human Resources and

Development Canada (HRDC) study cited in the text, which applies to people aged 15 to 64. Severity of disability is measured by determining loss of function associated with the disability and the number of disabilities the individual has. The percentage of total disabled in Table 4.1 was calculated by manipulating the "percentage of total number" category from the source data. We also use statistical information from the Society of Actuaries (SOA) 1985 Commissioner's Disability Tables. More recent studies were not available at the time of writing, but the underlying messages gleaned from these sources should reflect reality. Note that HRDC and SOA do not necessarily define "disability" in the same way. We also use information from CAIFA, CLHIA submissions, and the *Edmonton Journal*. As well, we use information from the Bureau des Service Financiers manual *Intermediaries in Insurance of Persons* (1999–2000). Another text that proved quite helpful was *Evaluating Disability Insurance*, by J. E. Figas (Toronto: CCH Canadian Limited, 1999).

Chapter 5: Automobile Insurance

This chapter relies heavily on information provided by the Insurance Bureau of Canada, Transport Canada, and the Department of Finance Canada. Information from individual provincial and territorial insurance regulators was used as well; please see "Information Resources" for contact information. In this chapter, we relate adverse selection and moral hazard, originally discussed in Chapter 1, to automobile insurance. The full reference to the *New England Journal of Medicine* article is "Effect of Eliminating Compensation for Pain and Suffering on the Outcome of Insurance Claims for Whiplash Injury," by J. David Cassidy, Linda J. Carroll, Pierre Côté, Mark Lemstra, Anita Berglund, and Åke Nygren, *NEJM* 342 (1996), 1179–86. The early-1930s criticism of the traditional insurance system that we refer to is a Columbia University proposal entitled "Columbia Univ. Council for Research in the Social Sciences Report by the Comm. to Study Compensation for Auto. Accidents" (1932) in the State Farm Insurance Company's *No-Fault Press Reference Manual* G-120 (1992).

Chapter 6: Property Insurance

This chapter relies heavily on information provided by the Insurance Bureau of Canada, Statistics Canada, and property insurance policies. The data cited on property crime refer to all breaking and entering and theft offences, not just those specifically related to private households. Also, while the crime data are from 2000, the census data are from 1996, the most recent year for which census data are available. Hence, our calculation of per household offences in Figure 6.4 does not entirely reflect the likelihood of a household experiencing the offence, but does give a flavour of the household-adjusted frequency of crime.

Chapter 7: Dealing with Your Insurance Company

We cite research from the *Journal of the American Medical Association*, *Group and Organization Management*, *Canadian Insurance*, and the *Journal of Business Ethics*. The citation that approximately 15% of all consumers choose insurance on the basis of price is from "Getting to Know the New Consumer," by B. French-Mullins, in *Canadian Insurance* (September 1997), 22. The information regarding A. M. Best methodologies is from the A. M. Best Company, 2001.

Chapter 8: Insurance Fraud

This chapter relies heavily on information provided by the Insurance Bureau of Canada (IBC), the Canadian Coalition Against Insurance Fraud (CCAIF), and the Investigative Services Division of the IBC. CCAIF also provides an annual "top ten" list of insurance frauds in Canada. While we recognize that material from industry organizations will obviously have an anti-fraud slant, they do play an important role in gathering and presenting facts, and their facts tend to be similar to results from other jurisdictions, such as the United States. Specific references for other studies and sources used appear in the chapter: these include *Canadian Underwriter* magazine, the *Journal of Insurance Regulation*, the *Review of Economics and Statistics*, and the *Financial Post*.

Glossary

Absolute liability — the requirement that insurance companies compensate innocent third parties, even when the first party has violated the insurance contract.

Accelerated living benefits — life insurance benefits that terminally ill policyholders are permitted to access while still living.

Accessibility criterion — the criterion in the Canada Health Act specifying that government health insurance coverage cannot be dependent upon user fees, health, or age.

Actual cash value — the value of damaged property minus an amount for appraised depreciation.

Adverse selection — a situation that occurs when asymmetric information problems exist, in which high-risk individuals, for whom the insurance policy is underpriced, obtain more insurance than low-risk individuals, for whom the insurance is overpriced.

Agent — an insurance intermediary who sells the products of one insurance company exclusively, in return for backup support provided by the company.

All-risks coverage — protection against all perils not specifically excluded in a property insurance policy; also known as comprehensive coverage.

Asymmetric information — a problematic situation in which the insurance company is unable to fully distinguish between high-risk and low-risk policyholders.

Basic coverage — protection against damage to the insured residence and personal property caused by specifically named perils; also known as named-perils coverage.

Broad coverage — property insurance coverage that provides basic coverage to personal property and comprehensive coverage to the insured residence.

Broker — an insurance intermediary who is not captive to a single insurance company, and who therefore has greater flexibility in terms of policies offered.

Build-up — inflation of damages associated with an otherwise valid claim.

Bylaw endorsement — an extension of a property insurance policy that provides protection against costs associated with complying with changes in construction codes and zoning bylaws.

Canada Health Act — legislation passed in 1984 setting forth the criteria and conditions that provinces and territories must satisfy in order to receive federal health transfer funds.

Canada Health and Social Transfer — the mechanism through which the federal government transfers funds to lesser jurisdictions in order to pay its portion of health care.

Cancellable contract — a disability insurance contract that allows the insurance provider to reserve the right to change the premiums and coverage, refuse renewal, or add exclusions or restrictions.

CCAIF — Canadian Coalition Against Insurance Fraud, an organization founded by insurance companies to fight insurance fraud.

Civil liability insurance — the term used in Quebec to describe liability insurance.

CLEAR system — Canadian Loss Experience Automobile Rating system, developed by the non-profit Vehicle Information Centre of Canada (VICC) and funded by the Canadian automobile insurance industry. The system ensures that insurance premiums reflect the propensity for specific autos to be damaged or stolen.

CLHIA — Canadian Life and Health Insurance Association of Canada, the national trade association of non-government life and health insurers.

CompCorp — Canadian Life and Health Insurance Compensation Corporation, an organization funded by member companies from the insurance industry that provides protection should a member company become insolvent.

Compensatory damages — funds awarded to a third party to reimburse actual costs associated with an incident as well as difficult-to-measure effects such as pain and suffering.

Comprehensive coverage — See all-risks coverage.

Comprehensiveness criterion — the criterion in the Canada Health Act specifying that government health insurance must insure all health services.

Condominium insurance — insurance designed to include only the parts of a property insurance package that condominium owners need.

Cost-of-living rider — a rider to a disability insurance contract that indexes benefits to inflation.

CPP — Canada Pension Plan.

Critical illness insurance — insurance that provides a lump-sum payment if the policyholder is diagnosed with one of a number of specific critical illnesses.

Depreciation — loss of value due to physical deterioration or obsolescence.

Direct compensation property damage insurance — insurance that allows the policyholder to collect directly from his or her own insurer should someone else damage his or her vehicle.

Direct seller — an insurance intermediary who sells insurance over the telephone, typically at a discount, to customers who respond to advertising.

Disability insurance — insurance that pays a monthly benefit if the policyholder is unable to work because of a disability.

EI — Employment Insurance (formerly Unemployment Insurance, or UI).

Elimination period — the period of time between the onset of a disability and the beginning of disability insurance benefits.

Expense approach — an approach by which one determines life insurance needs on the basis of future family expenses.

Experience good — a good that must be experienced before you can determine its worth, such as some health services.

Financial strength factors — a set of factors used to measure the strength of an insurance company's balance sheet and its ability to meet its debt obligations.

First party — the individual in whose name an insurance policy is issued; also referred to as the named insured.

Fixed immediate annuity — an immediate annuity with a fixed payout.

Fixed-term annuity — an annuity whose income payouts end after a fixed period; also known as a period-certain annuity.

Fraudster — someone who obtains money by deceiving people.

Group plan — an insurance contract between an insurance company and an entity representing a group, such as an employer or professional association.

Guaranteed renewable clause — a clause associated with insurance that permits renewability of the contract regardless of health status.

Guaranteed renewable contract — a disability insurance contract in which the insurer agrees not to modify the coverage or refuse renewability. The insurer can modify the premium only for an entire class of policyholders.

Guaranteed replacement cost — property insurance coverage that makes up the shortfall between 100% coverage and the actual cost of replacing the home or personal property.

IBC — the Insurance Bureau of Canada, which represents the P&C (property and casualty) insurance industry.

ICPB — Insurance Crime Prevention Bureau; the former name of the Investigative Services Division (ISD) of the Insurance Bureau of Canada.

Immediate annuity (IA) — a type of insurance in which an individual gives a non-refundable lump sum of money to an insurance company in exchange for a monthly or quarterly income stream; also known as longevity insurance or life annuity.

Incentive gap — the gap between the amount you earn by working and the amount you can receive from disability benefits.

Income approach — an approach by which one determines life insurance needs on the basis of income replacement.

Information condition — a condition in the Canada Health Act requiring jurisdictions to provide information to the federal minister of health about services provided.

Insurance fraud — any act or omission with a view to illegally obtaining an insurance benefit.

Interprovincial Agreement on Eligibility and Portability — an agreement between provinces regarding health insurance coverage.

Investigative systems — high-tech systems used to analyze databases for potential fraud.

ISD — Investigative Services Division of the Insurance Bureau of Canada; formerly known as the Insurance Crime Prevention Bureau (ICPB).

L&H — life and health insurance.

Legal liability — the requirement to compensate a third party for the first party's negligent behaviour.

Life annuity — See immediate annuity.

Life insurance — a type of insurance for which the policyholder pays a premium every month in exchange for a large payment to a beneficiary or the policyholder's estate upon death.

Longevity insurance — See immediate annuity.

Longevity risk — the risk of outliving one's resources.

Loss assessment coverage — optional coverage for condominium owners that protects against certain types of special insurance-related assessments by the condominium corporation.

Market profile factors — factors that measure an insurance company's ability to maintain a competitive advantage in the industry.

Master policy — the insurance policy held by a condominium corporation that covers damage to the entire structure, including each unit and common areas.

Medical mill — a group of health care professionals who use fraudulent billing practices to rip off patients and insurance companies.

Moral hazard — a situation in which an individual behaves recklessly, knowing that the insurance company can't observe the behaviour and that he or she will not incur the cost of the reckless behaviour.

Mortality credits — the difference between the return available in the market and the return earned by the survivors who hold a one-period life annuity contract.

Mortality swap — a tax strategy by which an individual invests in a life annuity and then uses the monthly benefits to fund a life insurance policy with a death benefit equivalent to the initial investment.

Named insured — the person in whose name an insurance policy is issued; also referred to as the first party.

Named perils coverage — See basic coverage.

No-fault insurance — an insurance system in which compensation is not paid out on the basis of fault. There is an effective cap on how much the insurance companies have to pay in most situations.

Non-cancellable contract — a disability insurance contract in which the insurer agrees not to change the premium and coverage until a specified age. See also guaranteed renewable contract.

Occupation — "Any occupation" refers to a disabled person's inability to work at any occupation for which he or she is qualified by education and experience. "Own occupation" refers to the disabled individual's inability to work at the job that he or she held before becoming disabled. "Regular occupation" refers to the disabled person's inability to work at a job within his or her profession.

Operating performance factors — factors that measure an insurance company's ability to generate income.

OSFI — the Office of the Superintendent of Financial Institutions, a federal regulatory body.

Owner's improvements — optional coverage for condominium owners that protects improvements to the unit.

P&C — property and casualty insurance.

PACICC — the Property and Casualty Insurance Compensation Corporation, an organization funded by Canadian insurance companies that pays pending claims should an insurance company go bankrupt.

Partial disability — a definition of disability that refers to a disabled individual's partial inability to work.

Participating annuity — an annuity in which holders are at risk (or stand to gain) if investment returns or mortality is worse (or better) than estimated.

Peril — an event that can cause a loss.

Period-certain annuity — See fixed-term annuity.

Permanent life insurance — a category of life insurance that contains a savings component; also known as whole life, universal life, or level life insurance.

Portability criterion — a criterion in the Canada Health Act specifying that the home province or territory continue to provide coverage for residents temporarily absent from the jurisdiction, or during a waiting period of up to three months after moving out of the jurisdiction.

Pre-disability indexing benefit — a rider to a disability insurance contract that automatically indexes benefits and premiums to changes in the policyholder's earnings.

Pre-existing condition — a condition that you already have before purchasing insurance.

Presumptive total disability — a definition of disability that refers to total or permanent loss of the use of a faculty or of certain limbs, resulting from disease or injury.

Private health insurance — health insurance coverage for financially burdensome, non-routine events as well as health services that are required on a routine basis, but not covered by public health insurance.

Property insurance — an insurance package that includes protection against perils and protection against personal legal liability.

Public administration criterion — a criterion in the Canada Health Act requiring that health care insurance be provided on a non-profit basis and be accountable to the provincial or territorial government.

Public health insurance — health insurance provided by the government that satisfies (and may surpass) the criteria and conditions set forth in the Canada Health Act; also known as Medicare.

Punitive damages — funds awarded to a third party to punish the first party and to deter both the third party and others from similar conduct.

QPP — Quebec Pension Plan.

Ratemaking — the process by which insurers determine risks and pricing for insurance.

Recognition condition — a condition in the Canada Health Act requiring a jurisdiction to publicize the fact that it has received federal contributions.

Red flag — a term used when analyzing a database to describe a variable value that suggests the need for caution.

Replacement costs — the costs associated with replacing lost or damaged property.

Residual disability — a definition of disability in which the disabled individual is able to work but suffers a decrease in income because of the disability.

Schedule — a list of specific valuables and their insured values in a property insurance contract.

Second party — the insurance company that issues the policy.

Soft-tissue damage — an injury to the soft tissue (for example, a sprain) that is difficult to diagnose objectively.

Statutory accident benefits — provision, independent of fault, for limited compensation to the driver and/or passengers of a vehicle for the financial burden associated with an accident.

Supplemental coverage — optional coverage for condominium owners that provides protection if the condominium corporation's master policy does not fully protect the unit.

Temporary life insurance — a life insurance contract for a specified period of time; also known as term life.

Tenant insurance — insurance designed to include only the components of a property insurance package that tenants need.

Tenant's improvements — coverage for improvements a tenant makes to his or her residence.

Term life insurance — See temporary life insurance.

Third party — a person with whom the first party might be involved in an accident.

Third party liability coverage — insurance coverage that enables compensation of a third party for the first party's negligent driving.

Total disability — a definition of disability in which the disabled individual is unable to work at all.

Travel insurance — insurance designed to overcome the gap between public health insurance coverage and the coverage required when travelling, meant to assist in dealing with emergencies associated with the trip.

Two-tiered health system — a health system in which some people get better health services than others, perceived by many Canadians as inequitable.

Uninsured automobile coverage — provision for limited compensation for a person injured or killed by an uninsured driver or unidentified vehicle.

Universality criterion — a criterion in the Canada Health Act specifying that all insured residents must be entitled to health services.

Variable immediate annuity — an immediate annuity with a variable payout.

Viatical settlement — an agreement whereby a terminally ill person can sell his or her rights under a life insurance policy to a third party in exchange for cash payments.

Viator — a terminally ill person who agrees to sell his or her rights under a life insurance policy to a third party in exchange for cash payments.

WCB — See workers' compensation board.

Workers' Compensation Board — a provincial or territorial board or commission that provides benefits for disabled workers; known by that name in most provinces, but also as the Workplace Safety and Insurance Board (Ontario), Workers' Compensation Health and Safety Board (Yukon), and Workplace Health, Safety and Compensation Commission (Newfoundland and Labrador).

About the Authors

Moshe A. Milevsky, Ph.D.

Moshe Milevsky is an Associate Professor of Finance at the Schulich School of Business at York University, and Executive Director of the Individual Finance and Insurance Decision (IFID) Centre, both in Toronto. He has a Ph.D. in finance (1996), an M.A. in mathematics and statistics (1992), and a B.A. in mathematics and physics (1990).

The focus of his teaching, research, and consulting work is the interplay between risk management, personal finance, and insurance. In addition to presenting keynote lectures, public seminars, and Ph.D., M.B.A., and B.B.A. courses at York University, he has worked as a consultant for many North American companies in the financial services industry. His clients have included ScotiaMcleod, AIM/Trimark, Investors Group, Merrill Lynch, Bank of Montreal, CIBC–Wood Gundy, Manulife Financial, American International Group (AIG), AXA Group, Keyport Insurance, Ibbotson Associates, TIAA-CREF, National Life, Principal Financial Group, and the State of Florida Board of Administration. In addition, he has provided expert testimony in a variety of court proceedings in both the United States and Canada.

Professor Milevsky has received numerous awards and research grants. They include grants from the Canadian Social Science and

Humanities Research Council (SSHRC), the Society of Actuaries, the International Certified Financial Planner Board of Standards, and the Canadian Investment Review Academic Sponsorship program. In 1996 he received the Financial Research Foundation's award for best Ph.D. dissertation in finance and the American Association of Individual Investors award for best paper in investment theory.

Professor Milevsky has published over 25 scholarly research articles in the *North American Actuarial Journal*, the *Journal of Risk and Insurance*, *Insurance: Mathematics and Economics*, *Risk* magazine, the *Journal of Financial and Quantitative Analysis*, and the *Journal of Derivatives*. He is co-editor of the *Journal of Pension Economics and Finance*, published by Cambridge University Press.

He is also the author of *Money Logic: Financial Strategies for the Smart Investor* (Stoddart, 1999) and *The Probability of Fortune: Financial Strategies with the Best Odds* (Stoddart, 2000) for the U.S. market. He has been cited in *Business Week*, the *Wall Street Journal*, the *New York Times*, *Barron's*, *Fortune*, and *Money* magazine, and he currently writes a monthly column for *National Post Business*.

Professor Milevsky is an avid soccer player and opera connoisseur. He lives in Toronto with his wife, Edna, and three daughters, Dahlia, Natalie, and Maya. You can visit Professor Milevsky's Web page at www.milevsky.com.

Aron A. Gottesman, Ph.D.

Aron Gottesman is an Assistant Professor of Finance at the Molson School of Business at Concordia University in Montreal and an Academic Research Member of the Individual Finance and Insurance Decision Centre in Toronto. He has a Ph.D. in finance (2001), an M.B.A. in finance and accounting (1997), and a B.A. in psychology (1994).

Professor Gottesman has taught graduate and undergraduate courses on investment analysis, derivative securities, and the theory of capital markets, and has presented corporate seminars on finance and risk-related topics. He has consulted extensively to both private corporations and governments in the areas of online finance education, portfolio analysis, insurance, and banking. Professor Gottesman has also created online courses for the financial services industry.

He has received a number of awards, research grants, and scholarships, including a research grant and doctoral fellowship from the Canadian Social Sciences and Humanities Research Council (SSHRC), an Ontario Graduate Scholarship, research grants from Concordia University, and scholarships from York University. In 2001 he received an award for the best paper on financial institutions at the Northern Finance Association Meetings.

Professor Gottesman's research interests are financial intermediation, asset pricing, and market microstructure. He has published a number of refereed journal articles, including publications in the *Journal of Financial Markets and Financial Review*. He has also presented working papers at numerous professional meetings and seminars.

Professor Gottesman is a professionally trained musician. He lives in Montreal with his wife, Ronit, daughter, Libby Leah, and sons, Yakov Tzvi and Raphael Yehudah. You can visit Professor Gottesman's Web page at www.arongottesman.com.

Index

INDEX